A HAN
ON SUPPLY
CHAIN
MANAGEMENT

A PRACTICAL BOOK WHICH QUICKLY COVERS BASIC CONCEPTS & GIVES EASY TO USE METHODOLOGY AND METRICS FOR DAY-TO-DAY PROBLEMS, CHALLENGES AND AMBIGUITY FACED BY EXECUTIVES IN DECISION MAKING

KULDEEPAK SINGH

INDIA · SINGAPORE · MALAYSIA

Notion Press

No. 8, 3rd Cross Street,
CIT Colony, Mylapore,
Chennai, Tamil Nadu – 600 004

First Published by Notion Press 2021
Copyright © Kuldeepak Singh 2021
All Rights Reserved.

ISBN 978-1-63850-887-8

Contents

Preface

As a Logistics and Supply Chain Professional, it was everyday affair to deal with dynamics of the trade and overcome problems with best possible outcome. Experimentation with lot of concepts to handle complexities of the operations was a tedious but necessary task. While dealing with tricky and ambiguous situations the first thing which always came to mind was to refer some guidebook quickly, but it was always challenging to go back on the reading desk and look for the relevant book having the suitable topic. Most of the books are too elaborative in nature and full of theories with little practical insights and few are even missing practical applications cum solutions for the risk assessment, decision making or bringing visibility in supply chain.

Being Supply chain practitioner himself, one always floundered to have such reference material at work desk to be referred quickly before getting involved to drawing board and design solutions especially at the Executive and Managerial level.

This QuickBook solves the problem to a large extent and contains successfully applied solutions and gives a refreshed look on the concepts which are there but in scattered form.

The book is conceived with a view to give basic concepts and provide practical approach in easy and comprehensible manner for decision making. Primary aim is to benefit existing Logistics and Supply chain professionals but its beneficial for student pursuing Certificate and Diploma courses on the subject to peek insight practical approaches before they enter in professional world. Also, it can be used to train managers who are NOT involved in Supply Chain and Logistics activity for quick insights and better understanding on the subject matter.

About the Author

Mr Kuldeepak Singh is a supply chain professional with a rich experience of a decade and half. He has handled multiple portfolios during his tenure and worked with many organizations like Hindustan Latex Limited, Godrej & Boyce Mfg. Co. Ltd to name a few. His expertise domain includes Optimizing Secondary and Last Mile Logistics, Process Mapping, Cost Optimization, Operational Excellence, Productivity Improvement and Warehousing (RFQ to Operations Initiation) in Consumer Durables, FMCG Sector and Healthcare Domain. Apart from this he has consultant level proficiency for Supply Chain in Health projects which he gained while working with one of biggest and oldest government health project Revised National Tuberculosis Control Project-II (RNTCP-II) and other Government projects.

His educational background includes M.Sc. (Mathematics), PGDBM in Marketing Management, & Diploma in Material Management. He is Six Sigma Green Belt Certified professional from Indian Statistical Institute. His on-the-job work roles provided him rich exposures in audit domain (includes ISO-9001:2015 and FoSCoS), Project Management Office & Digital Initiatives.

Basics of Supply Chain Management

1.1 Definition

Supply chain is a concept which can be defined as an interconnected system which consists the network of **physical and virtual flow of goods and services** to satisfy the customer demand as per their desired service levels and at optimum cost.

Physical flow can be categorized as People, Raw materials, finished goods through one or other means for facilitating the movement within or outside organization.

Virtual flow can be classified as flow of the cash and management information systems defined to ensure low risk and deviation from set objectives and ensure maximum visibility to the management for the decision making.

1.2 Supply Chain or Demand Chain

When we say Supply Chain it implies that the origin of the movement is triggered by the manufacturer or service provider but as the concept matured another thought started that movement or flow starts when there is need for the goods or service from the consumers. In other words when there is demand then the flow will take place and so the other associated activities.

Supply Chain and Demand Chain are basically two sides of the same coin and identical ones. An organization has the choice to define strategies based on to generate business. In technical terms one can go for PUSH strategy or PULL strategy for meeting the customer requirements

PARAMETERS	SUPPLY CHAIN	DEMAND CHAIN
CAPITAL FLOWS	Cost drives the decision	Cash flow and profitability are important
OBJECTIVE	Focus on operational planning	Focus on demand generation from market
PERIOD	Short term goals	Long term goals
PLANNING	Focus on execution	Focus on delivering value
EFFICIENCY	Focus on high efficiency	Focus on effectiveness
RISK	Risk Averse	Calculated Risk

Exhibit-1: Difference Between Supply chain and Demand Chain

Author's Tip- For easy recall keep in mind the COPPER Matrix to understand the dynamics of the business in practical situation

1.3 Types of Supply Chain

Supply Chain strategy can vary from business to business and sector to sector, but they can be largely categorised in **four types**:

   a. **INTEGRATED MAKE-TO STOCK-MODEL (MTS):** Normally, a significant no of companies follows this model to ensure that they have the real time visibility of demand thru ERP and the products are stored in such a way that stocks out doesn't happen. Based on dynamics of market and inputs, MRP (Material Requirement Planning), production plans and schedules can be aligned to meet the requirements.

e.g.- FMCG companies like P&G, HUL, Godrej works on this model as they have multiple distribution channels like retail shops, Online, Canteens, Supermarkets and Malls etc

b. **BUILT TO ORDER (Make to Order-MTO):** Its fast-paced model wherein the product is built almost immediately upon the receipt of order and send onwards for supply. It requires high level of inventory planning and model support the mass customization concept.

e.g. Dell Computers is the perfect example for such type of supply chain. It delivers to personalized product to each customer within defined timelines.

c. **CONTINUOUS REPLENISHMENT MODEL (Make to Availability-MTA):** Alternatively called as Make-to-availability Model ensure consistent replenishment of the stocks to ensure stocks our based-on demand from various customer segments. TOC (Theory of Constraints) is one such tool to implement such type of models which has gained popularity among companies.

e.g.- ABB, Tata Steel, Titan & Liberty are few of the organizations who work on this model

d. **CHANNEL ASSEMBLY MODEL:** The model is equivalent to Make to Stock but with one added leg in the process. The products parts or material is received at a 3PL partner aligning strategically to assemble and distribute further.

e.g.- Tata Salt sends the salt bags in bulk from their salt refining units to various 3PL partners across the country where they refill in small pouches of 1 kg or higher and dispatch it further to various channel partners assigned to their area of operations. Ingram Micros is another fine example for the CAM model

> **Author's Tip-** To recall easily keep in mind the **CA-M-OSA (Channel Assembly, Make To- Order, Stock & Availability)**

1.4 Wastages and Inefficiencies in Supply Chain

Any activity or process which does not add value to the customer is called a wastage and will lead to inefficiencies. Wastages and inefficient supply chain may lead to disastrous outcomes.

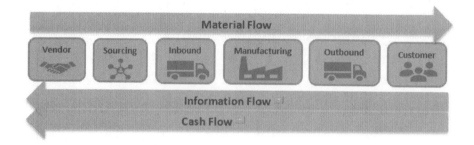

Exhibit-2: MICA flow Diagram in Supply Chain

Supply chain **WASTAGES and INEFFICIENCIES** arising out from the activity can be categorized primarily in **8 types (8W's of Wastages)**:

a. **Transportation:** Any unwanted movement of materials or product is a form of waste. Damages happening from movement is inefficiency arising from the activity

b. **Inventory:** Raw material Storage, Work in progress Inventory, Finished Goods storage is an act of waste. Obsolescence and Cost of Holding inventory is inefficiency arising from the activity.

c. **Movement/Motion:** Every mile travel of materials lead to cost and is form of waste Unnecessary and complicated motion can cause harm to employees, damages to equipment, or can create defects in the product which is the inefficiency happening from the activity.

d. **Waiting:** Wait time for the material or downtime during production is unnecessary wastage. Cost incurred on wastage of productive hour is one the inefficiency generated by this situation.

e. **Over Production:** When production **exceeds** the customer demands it creates additional material to be stored or transported which is the inefficiency due to this decision.

f. **Over processing:** A product or service having more attributes or capabilities than desired by company or remains unused by the customer is considered wastage. Processes and tasks defined for such attributes is the inefficiency generated due to this.

g. **Defects:** Defects are attributed to product quality which does not meet the defined standards from the company and needs to be scrapped or reworked. Additional cost and efforts must be deployed for taking corrective is the inefficiency due to deviation.

h. **Non-Utilized Talent/Skills-** Underutilized skills of an employee deployed for the task/activity is the waste in the process. It leads to demotivation and high cost having less productivity is the inefficiency generated by the wrong fit.

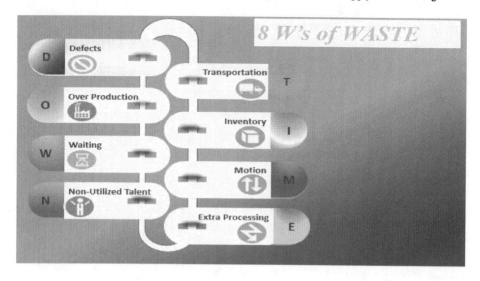

Exhibit-3: 8W's of Waste in Supply Chain

Author's Tip- To recall easily keep in mind the TIMWOODS or DOWNTIME abbreviation

1.5 Metrics to Measure the Effciency

In order to make better, informed and quick decisions in VUCA (Volatile, Uncertain, Complex, Ambiguous) world, we need measurable, time -saving, easy to interpret and most importantly decision assisting key performance indicators with better Actionable Insights. Key Metrics to measure the supply chain can be as follows-

Quality Indicators	Financial Indicators
Cash to Cash Cycle Time	Turn -Earn Index (TEI)
Perfect Order Management	Gross Margin ROI
Supply Chain Cycle Time	Total Supply Chain Cost

1. Cash to Cash Cycle Time

Definition

Cash to cash measures the amount of time operating capital is tied up. During this time cash is not available for other purposes. A fast cash to cash indicates a lean and profitable supply chain

Formula

Cycle Time (In Days) =*Materials payment date – customer order payment date*

- *Average for all orders for a week, month, quarter to be calculated.*
- *Weighted average materials payment date can be calculated as Final Product requires several materials or inputs*

2. Perfect Order Management

Definition

The Perfect Order Measure calculates the error-free rate of each stage for a Purchase Order (e.g.- error in order forecasting for procurement, error in warehouse pickup process, error in invoicing and error in shipping orders etc.)

Formula

Perfect Orders = *(Total orders – Erratically executed orders)/total orders) * 100*

3. Supply Chain Cycle Time

Definition

Supply chain cycle time indicates the overall efficiency of the supply chain. Short cycles make a more efficient and agile supply chain.

Formula

Supply Cycle Time- *Sum of the longest lead times for each stage of the cycle*

4. Turn -Earn Index (TEI)

Definition

TEI is measured to ensure balance for SKU or brands generating low margins have high Inventory Turns (Refer Chapter -3 for details) and the medium or High Margin SKU or brands with low Inventory turns have high margings

Formula

Turn- Earn Index: (Inventory turns) x (Gross Profit %) x 100.

5. Gross Margin ROI

Definition

Gross margin return on investment is the gross profit margin earned on every rupee invetment on inventory. It gives measurement of SKU or Brand which produces more gross profit from the Inventory.

Formula

GMROI: [Gross Profit]/[(Opening Stock-Closing Stock)/2] X 100

6. *Total Supply Chain Cost*

Definition

Total Supply chain cost is calculated to understand the end-to-end cost factors involved i.e. from Material procurement to Customer Delivery. It consists of primarily five cost which is related to material, Manpower, Inventory Holding, Logistics and Overhead expenses

Formula

TSCC = Material Cost +Manpower Cost+ Inv. Holding cost+
Logistics Cost + Overheads
(More complex Calculation will add Quality conformance cost, Delay Cost, Lead Time cost etc.)

> **Author's Tip- To recall Supply Chain Metrics easily keep in mind PCS (Quality Indicators) - Perfect Order management, C2C Cycle, Supply Chain Cycle Time**
> **TGT (Cost Indicators) — Turn Earn Index, Gross Margin ROI, TCSS**

1.6 Building a Resilient Supply Chain

There is no magic formula but measure, monitor and improve will make wonders in the supply chain efficiency. **Visibility, flexibility, and agility to alter the course at lesser cost and without service level disruption is key to the most complex problem.** As explained above an organization or an individual must keep sharp focus in reducing the wastages and inefficiencies as much as possible and improve every bit of it. Few questions a supply chain leader must ask-

    a. *Is disruption strategy in place?*
    b. *How quickly the supply chain can be restored in wake of Disruption?*

    c.   *Are teams trained, prepared, and empowered to handle the change?*

Resilience is not only to sustain but to take correctives if disruption takes place. In the current business scenario where shortened life cycle of product, demand supply gaps, longer global supply chains moreover affected by weather, social, political and economic disturbances have become more common things than ever. So, building a robust and sustainable supply chain is not an option but necessity.

Logistics Management

2.1 Definition

Any event of physical flow and related activities in the supply chain can be defined as Logistics. Resources may involve people, equipment, infrastructure, and information flow which forms Logistics ecosystem.

"Logistics management is that part of supply chain management that plans, implements, and controls the efficient, effective forward and reverses flow and storage of goods, services and related information between the point of origin and the point of consumption in order to meet customers' requirements" (CSCMP Definition)

Logistics management basically involves planning, execution and control of Transportation including Third Party Logistics and Fourth Party Logistics, Warehousing, inventory management at all levels i.e. Operational, Tactical and Strategic.

Logistics and Supply Chain Management:

In simple terms Logistics is Subset of Supply chain. In another words, Logistics activities are part of Supply Chain Management but not vice versa.

Supply Chain works to bring competitive edge to the organization while Logistics focuses on meeting the requirement of customers.

2.2 Transportation

The process of moving goods from one point to another point can be referred as **transportation. It must be safe, reliable, and sustainable and cost efficient.**

Modes of Transportaion

Mode of transportation can be broadly categorized in **four** parts
1. **Road Transport** *(Road/Rail/Pipeline)*
2. **Water Transport** *(Waterways cum Shipping)*
3. **Air Transport** *(Flight/Drones)*
4. **Hybrid Model** -Combination of above two or more (**Piggyback or TFCC**-*Trailer on flatcar/***COFC**-*Container of Flat Car/***RORO**-*Roll on Roll Off/***FISHY Back/BIRDY Back**)

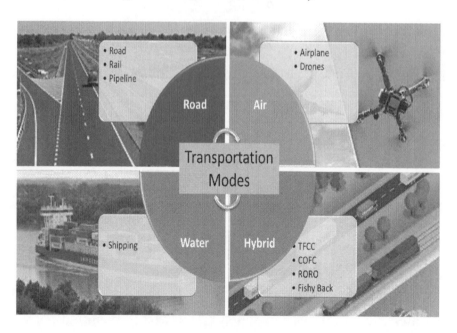

Exhibit-4: Transportation Modes

LOGISTICS SEGMENTATION- Segmentation can be done on various factors like

1. **Industry based** *(e.g.- Telecom/Coal/Steel/Consumer Electronics/ Pharma etc.),*
2. **Product type basis** *(e.g.- Food vs Non-Food and Perishable vs Non-Perishable etc.)*
3. **Customer Basis** *(e.g.- Retail vs Institutional)*
4. **Technical requirements** (e.g.- *Cold chain vs Normal*)

2.3 Comparative Analysis Between Transportaion Modes

Comparative analysis gives a clear visibility of various modes of transportation based on various factors like Cost, Lead Time (Time taken to reach from source point to Destination Point), Reach (Accessibility to geographical Area), Flexibility (To be used in various capacity, industries, technical requirements or as a mix of all) etc.

A comparative matrix given above gives a clear picture on the various factors to be considered before deciding the right mode or mix of mode to achieve efficient, reliable and sustainable design for the organization.

COMPARISON OF TRANSPORTATION MODES						
Factors	ROAD	Rail	Pipeline	WATER	AIR	Drones
• COST	• Medium	• Low	• Low	• Low	• High	• High
• LEAD TIME	• Low	• Medium	• Medium	• High	• Low	• Low
• RELIABLE	• High	• Medium	• High	• Low	• High	• High
• CAPACITY (To Carry)	• Medium	• Medium	• High	• High	• Low	• Low
• REACH	• High	• Medium	• Low	• Low	• Low	• High
• FLEXIBILTY	• High	• Medium	• Low	• Low	• Low	• High
• INDUSTRY/ PRODUCTS	• Consumer Products/ Retails	• Coal Steel Fertilizer	• Oil	• Volumetric Products	• Critical Products	• Evolving

Exhibit-5 Comparison of Transportation Modes

Author's Tip- To design the mode give weightage to top factors which is aligned with your USP of business model and select the mode of Transportation. Let's see this by an example – Less Lead time, Low cost and High Reach is priority in the order for consumer products company (Retail). TM can be decided quickly-

e.g. Priority 1- Less Lead Times (Option 1-Air, Option -2 Rail & Option-3 Road)

Priority 2 -Low Cost (Options 1- Rail & Option 2- Road)

Priority 3 -High Reach (Road) – Final Decision should be Road

2.4 Optimizing Logistics Cost vis-à-vis Service Level

Logistics activity is the one the biggest cost factor in the Supply Chain. Cost incurred on the flow of goods is under constant scrutiny to optimize. Decisions makers normally tend to look at the Transport vendors for reducing and optimizing the cost as a short term which is not a winning strategy and leads to a complex negotiation. We must review and realign other factors to remove inefficiencies and Achieve a Right Cost for a defined service level. There are various factors to be looked at for an efficient and Cost effective.

  a. **Logistic Network Redesign:** As a proactive approach one must follow *"Design for Logistics"* strategy from the very beginning stage of Product development else keep reviewing the logistics arrangement and take correctives to optimize. Basic three things to be kept in mind:

  1. Packaging Requirements for safer delivery at lesser Cost including **Re-usage**
  2. Transportation arrangement for Cost optimization (**Mode Mix**)

3. Process Realignment like converting *Sequential Processes to Concurrent Processes* to ensure speed and reduced lead time

b. **Vendor Management:** Map the vendor Strength vs Available. Calculate various modes with respect to control and sustain. Primary decisions points to be considered:

1. Self-managed or 3rd party Managed (3PL/4PL)
2. Define Capacity Required vs Capacity Strength of Vendors by optimizing transportation mode including variable factors like Seasonality, Skewness and likely Disruption in the Vendor, based on products/goods

    (Refer Annexure -1 Calculation sheet format for identifying Primary and Secondary dispatches and strength mapping as an exercise)

c. **Service Levels Requirements:** Sustaining the business and counter competition minimum service levels have to be defined and ensure the following to achieve

1. **Design Mix for Transportation** -Owned Vehicles vs Outsourced Vehicles (Leased for Fixed term or on call basis (e.g. 40:40:20 ratio – Owned 40%: Leased for fixed term 40%: On call basis 20%)
2. **Payment Terms** based on Performance Clause and inbuilt penalty to guarantee minimum service levels {Advance Payment ratio/Work Completion pay Ratio/ Performance Reward and Penalty (Fixed or % Basis)
3. **Transit Time** – A very critical and important factor in determining the service levels vis-a vis cost. A traditional approach to defining transit time is an average time taken from one mode or mix of modes, but it must be looked in much broader perspective. Transit time can be categorized based on various timelines and decision to

be taken to follow a broad spectrum to ensure minimum commitment levels are met with respect to transit times.

    a. **Maximum Transit Time** – Highest time to reach destination.

    b. **Minimum Transit Time** – Shortest time taken to reach destination.

    c. **Optimistic Transit Time** – Best case scenario happened based on historic data.

    d. **Pessimistic Transit Time** – Worst Case scenario based on historic data.

    e. **Normal Transit Time** – Averaged out scenario based on historic data.

    f. **Optimal Transit Time** – Best performed scenario based on Historic data.

*(**Lead Time is normally used synonymously as transit time but** lead times is the total time taken from Planning to Serve time to Customer including Returns, however the transit time is the amount of time taken to travel the distance from point of origin to point of delivery. To summarize the terms, **we can say that Transit time is subset of Lead time**)*

d. **Breaking Down the Process Cost:** One of the most challenging and cumbersome tasks is to bring visibility in the overall process and associated costs in supply chain. Transportation being one the major cost factor brings multiple challenges being exposed to VUCA world.

To overcome the problem, we must breakdown the transportation in various ***processes and costs associated with each activity like Receipt, Unloading, Storage, Picking, Loading, Documentation and Return.*** One can follow Activity Based costing and Pareto Analysis to prioritize the focus area and controlling the deviation.

(Refer details on calculation of the activities in our Metrics and Measurement section in simplistic way for monitoring)

e. **Responsiveness and Flexibility:** Logistics must be as cost effective and equally responsive as well to change. It must be predesigned and capable of switching based on market dynamics. It may be sudden demand of specific product or demand skewness in a geography or change in ratio of B2C and B2B business. Transportation must be flexible enough to respond to such demand swiftly.

> **Author's Tip- To inbuilt Responsiveness and Flexibility, SHABD method can be used to measure and further strengthened by DIGROM Approach**

S-H-A-B-D (Single Hour Arrangement Based on Demand) can be defined as a standard method to gauge the flexibility and responsiveness. How many hours it takes to respond and reduce the time over a period based on business patterns to maintain standard level of service. Single hour is not about an hour, but it must not go into double digit of hours and need to be done without affecting existing throughput and service levels. It helps in reducing one of the important wastage area i.e. **Wait Time.**

To ensure **SHABD** implementation one should follow **DIGROM** approach-

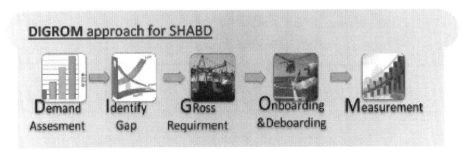

Exhibit-6: Diagrom Flow

a. **Demand Assessment** -Assess seasonality/Festivity/Special Sales Schemes related demand pattern apart from normal transportation requirements.

Demand Assessment is very critical and forecasting with the help of predictive like usage of based qualitative methods and quantitative methods:

Qualitative Methods:

1. **Delphi Technique** – An expert panel assess the demand individually and meet to discuss and realign each. Such meeting keeps on happening till they all near consensus.
2. **Market Research** – Mostly outsourced to expert organizations specialized in the job. They survey the potential geography and potential segment to reach conclusion. (*Mostly done for new product category to assess the preference, sentiments, and economic status of customers*)
3. **Sales Force Opinion – Sales Team** is asked to provide the expected demand from their region and the demand is aggregated and summarized to final figures after realignment.

Quantitative Methods:

1. **Trend Projection Method** – It primarily takes the secondary data available for the past demand for 2-3 years and extrapolation is done thru Time series to assess demand for coming period.
2. **Econometric Models** – Most popular one in econometric model is single equation-based Regression Model. It can be single variable demand function like Use of Ink based on pens sold or tea/coffee selling is linked to population in the region etc or multiple demand variable like demand of vegetables is linked population, household purchasing power, alternative products available.

3. **Barometric Technique-** This method considers of economic factors with statistical tools to predict demand The technique works on recording statistical analysis tools like Leading Indicators, Coincident Indicators or Lagging Indicators to forecast demand. E.g.- Women's/Girl hostels demand can be linked to girls enrolled to schools and no of women's working region though the major drawback is the precision lacks.

b. **Identify The Gap-** Measure Capacity of Existing Setup of Vendor Base **(Refer 2.4 b)** and their Capacity Constraints based on route/ Geography/Type of Business (Retail/Institutional/Technical requirements etc) to define the Gap between Skewness and Normal Demand.

*(In statistical way we can define **control charts based on required parameters** which needs to be monitored **e.g.**- Route wise Average, Max and Minimum cubic capacity/No of trucks -type wise utilized for transportation thru road mode in last two years can be plotted. Analysing the charts will give clear indication when the maximum defined tolerance limit got breached against forecasted. Following the pattern of such deviations we can easily identify the gap **Refer Chapter 6 for Control Charts)***

c. **Gross Requirement Review** - Review the transportation MIX/ Vendor Base needs to be used for catering the new volume and realign to manage the capacity based on Total Demand on Zero Based Planning concept *(For Quick Decision refer **Author Tips of Clause 2.3** Comparative Analysis of Transportation Modes)*

*(While reviewing the prime focus must be the strategic goal of the organization or business model being followed **i.e.**- Product differentiation, cost leadership or Niche marketing. This will give clear direction on managing/optimizing the basic dilemma of cost vis-a-vis service in best way)*

d. **ON Boarding/Deboarding**-RFQ/Negotiation/Boarding must be done before hand preferably at the beginning of Financial Year to address the gap. (Min Business Volume can be assured to vendor vis-a vis desired service levels commitment to be guaranteed by vendor at effective cost). Onboarding can be done for short term/ long term or Project Basis as well. We must be open and transparent with vendor on the terms of contract and commitment of business esp. in case of short term.

Pre-Requisites/Checklist for Vendor Onboarding: Onboarding Checklist may primarily consist of compliances, Authenticity, strength in terms of asset, finances and manpower, authenticity of vendor itself, Segment strength and clienteles, Credit terms, competency in terms of rate and Service levels, Digital strength for collaboration and internal management. Hereby giving a sample snapshot for **Road Transportation** which can be used and customized to suit the requirements-

	ON BOARDING CHECKLIST	
Factors to be checked	☐ Registered as Goods carrier with RTO	
	☐ Complied with GSTN	☐ Individual Owner
	☐ Financial Strength	☐ Pvt Ltd Comapny
	☐ Asset Heavy or Light	☐ Public Ltd Company
	☐ Commision Agent	☐ 3PL
	☐ 4 PL	☐ Veh Strength< 5 veh
	☐ ....Staff Strength	☐ Veh Strength > 5 Veh
	☐ Documents of veh(s)	☐ Office Address Proof
	☐ ...Years of Experience	☐ Segement expertise (...)
	☐ Clientele List	☐ Recommendation/Commendation letter
	☐ Credit terms	☐ Market Credibility -Not
	☐ Rate List compatability	☐ SLA Commitment
	☐ Softwares used for visibility and MIS	

e.   **Measure to Manage-** Performance review to be done based on committed volumes and service levels. Repeat the process to synchronise and reduce SHABD time.

(Refer Section 2.5 Metrics to measure)

2.5 Metrics to Measure the Performance

Metrics is a quantifiable process which considers measurements of current and pasts to define success and promotes continuous improvement as well.

It can be defined and categorized based on various Indicators:

a.   **Quality Indicators-** *How well the task has been performed?*

b.   **Response Time Indicators-***How much time it takes to complete task?*

c.   **Financial/Cost Indicators-***How much it costs to perform the task?*

d.   **Productivity Indicators-***How effective the resources are used to do the task?*

Quality	Responsiveness	Financial/Cost	Productivity
% of Perfect Execution	Average Shipment Loading/Unloading	Average Transportation Cost	Vehicle Capacity Utilization
On time / Before Time Delivery	Average Lead Time	Cost to Sales Ratio	Route Planning & Optimization
Total Travel between two Accidents	Vehicle Turnaround time	Fuel vs Veh. Running Cost Ratio	Vehicles Uptime

Logitics performance can be measured based on these parameters given below:

Quality Indicators
1. % of Perfect Execution from Total Order
Definition

It measures the percentage of consignments/shipments reaching to the end point in perfect condition i.e. without damages due to transit handling, travel conditions like rain, poor roads, loss of package during travel etc

Formula

$$\text{\% of Perfect Order Execution} = \frac{\text{No. of Consignments reached without damages/shortages}}{\text{Total No of Shipments Dispatched or Received}} * 100$$

2. On time/Before Time Delivery
Definition

This measures the percentage of total consignments/shipments reached On time/Before time. In other words, the lead time compliance % for all the shipments dispatched or received

Formula

$$\text{\% Lead time compliance} = \frac{\text{No of Consignments reached without delay}}{\text{Total No of Consignments Dispatched or Received}} * 100$$

3. Total Travel between two Accidents
Definition

The criteria measure the safer travel of goods and gives indication about the patterns leading to accidents. It may be specific route, bad roads or human error due to driver

Formula

Safer distance travelled without accident $=\dfrac{\text{Total Distance Travelled}}{\text{Total No of Accidents}}$

Responsiveness Indicators

1. Average Shipment Loading/Unloading Time

Definition

The measurement is done to analyse the average time taken to unload or Load shipments. This can be further categorized based on shipment type, warehouse wise, route wise, product type wise for further insights.

Formula

Average Shipment Loading/ Unloading Time $=\dfrac{\text{Total hours taken to load/unload in a time period}}{\text{Total No. of Shipments}}$

2. Average Lead Time

Definition

Average Transit time/delivery time/Lead Time can be measured to identify the serve time (Hours/Days) to end point from the time shipment left the start point from manufacturing point, warehouse or supplier facility. It can be further categorized based on route, location or type of end point being served. Normally the time period is taken for one year to compare with previous service levels and/or for competitive benchmarking

Formula

Average Transit Time $=\dfrac{\text{Total hours/days taken from dispatch point to deliver point for all shipments period}}{\text{Total No. of Shipments}}$

3. Vehicle Turnaround time

Definition

One of the most critical factors esp. for vendor satisfaction/driver's satisfaction and gauge the effectiveness of the internal processes' s swiftness. It can be calculated as Idle time spent at the facility between arrival and departure.

Formula

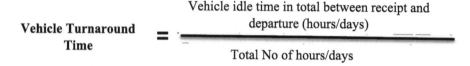

$$\text{Vehicle Turnaround Time} = \frac{\text{Vehicle idle time in total between receipt and departure (hours/days)}}{\text{Total No of hours/days}}$$

Financial/cost Indicators

1. Average Transportation Cost

Definition

Average transportation cost per km is significant measure on the cost incurred on movement of goods. It can be measured on volume/unit or per unit basis. This cost can be further classified on Product group basis, Geographical area/route wise basis. It gives a good on hand information for negotiation for rates with 3PL or 4PL service providers and can be used to evaluate them as well

Formula

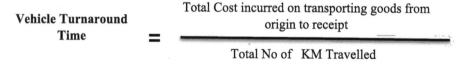

$$\text{Vehicle Turnaround Time} = \frac{\text{Total Cost incurred on transporting goods from origin to receipt}}{\text{Total No of KM Travelled}}$$

2. Cost to Sales Ratio

Definition

Percentage spend on transporting the goods against the total Sales value is defined as Cost to Sales (CTS) Ratio. It provides a good insight for analysis comparison and budgeting exercise. Cost of transportation must include primary movement and secondary including overheads to arrive at actual cost.

Formula

$$\text{Cost to Sales Ratio} = \frac{\text{Total Cost incurred on transporting goods from origin to receipt}}{\text{Total Value of Goods Sold}}$$

3. Fuel vs Veh. Running Cost Ratio

Definition

Fuel being a major component (35-45%) in Vehicle running cost. Organizations having Owned/Fixed Lease vehicles with Fuel being high variable component plays a pivotal role. Keeping a tab on Fuel Cost vs total Vehicle running cost is good measure for controlling the overhead expenses as well as get benefit if fuel price reduces.

Formula

$$\text{Fuel to Vehicle Running Ratio} = \frac{\text{Total Fuel Cost incurred in a month}}{\text{Total Vehicle Running Cost ((Leased Cost + Fuel Cost)}} * 100$$

Productivity Indicators

1. Vehicle Capacity Utilization

Definition

This parameter measures the vehicle capacity utilization against the ideal capacity in required time (Monthly/Quarterly/Annually). It can be further classified into Vehicle type wise, Primary vs Secondary transportation, Route wise etc for granular detailing. It can be measured in Cubic Feet utilization or Units accommodated (For Box in Box out transactions) against standard capacity.

Formula

$$\text{Vehicle Capacity Utilization Ratio} = \frac{\text{Cubic Ft of goods Transported or Total Units Transported}}{\text{Total Cubic Ft or Standard Units capacity of Vehicles}} * 100$$

2. Route Planning & Optimization

Definition

Route Optimization is very critical, and measuring is complex phenomenon as well. Route planning must be done scientifically (Like using methods **North West Corner Rule, Least Cost Method or Vogel's approximation method**) or with the help of software to reduce travel and so the cost. Effective planning can be measured from average no of stops planned per km for a period of measurement (Monthly/Quarterly or Annually) in LTL (Less than Truck Loads) cases. **e.g.-** MRO (Maintenance, Repair and Overhaul) business. For more insight's vehicle type wise/route wise data can be explored for improving efficiencies esp. in circular route plans (To and Fro both ways). Higher the number better the efficiency.

Formula

$$\text{Stoppages per Km} = \frac{\text{Total Stops Covered in a month}}{\text{Total KM travelled by Vehicle(s) in a month}}$$

3. Vehicles Uptime

Definition

E- commerce and retail business surge has led to organizations opting for leased vehicle on per kilometre travel basis or monthly fixed distance to be covered with certain riders from such vehicles. It may be minimum points to be covered to Fixed charge per day plus points covered etc. Leased vehicles availability must be maximum to ensure minimum service levels as it comes normally at higher cost in comparison to vehicles deployed for FTL deliveries. Absenteeism defeats the overall objective for opting this model.

Formula

$$\% \text{ Downtime of Vehicles} = \frac{(\text{Total No. of Working Days} - \text{No. of Days Absent})}{\text{Total No. of working days in period}} * 100$$

2.6 Managing the Disruption-factors & Strategy to Counter

A brief introduction to the topic focusing on events which logistics managers identify as uncertainty or shifting patterns and is direct threat to the sustainable business model, even potential to close the business itself. Disruption must be accounted while designing strategies and logistics decision makers must keep tab on such trends for profitability and business continuity. Key disruptors in current times can be classified as **MARGS**

Exhibit-7: Disruption Factors -MARGS

a. **MASS CUSTOMIZATION**- In other words Built- to- Order (Refer Clause 1.3) for masses. Continuous rise in Purchasing power fuelled with awareness due to ever highest reach of internet facility has led to demand of personalization at low cost and some industries adapted *"Lot size of One"* in true sense. This has led to serious disruption in the way transportation is done. The products may differ in size, weight, volume, varied attributes of handling may lead to serious inefficiencies in cost to serve.

(For details read *Mass Customization: The New Frontier in Business Competition* (Harvard Business Review Press, 1992))

b.   **AMAZON EFFECT-** New age business models like Amazon and Flipkart has fired up the expectations of the customers. Now the customers expect agile, flexible, and responsive delivery partners at lesser cost. Organizations are under tremendous pressure to match and manage the service levels. To fulfil the expectations to some extent the way is either ramp up technologically or leverage the supply chain of new e-commerce players.

c.   **RISE OF MACHINES-** Multiple frontiers of disruption has been opened whether Predictive Data Analysis, Machine Learning, Robotics and Automation, Self-Driven Vehicles, 3D Printing lead customized delivery model, Blockchain, Augmented reality, Mobile Apps based tracking, wearables etc has led to requirement for new resources, roles like CDO (Chief Digital Officer), CAO (Chief Automation Officer) but in totality lesser human resources. Companies must optimize and build collaborative platforms for getting best of both humans and machine.

d.   **GREEN ENERGY-** Fossil fuels are finite resources and as per DHL sustainability report we may be in serious trouble regarding availability of fossil fuels by 2040. World has taken up to alternate fuel sources whether Solar Energy, Electricity, Hydrogen fuel cells, Biomass etc. They are in nascent stage, but development is on fast lane. Alternate fuels are comparatively better in terms of cost and less carbon emission ensures lesser pollution to environment. At strategic level one must start looking for them and start deploying gradually

e. **START UPS** – Newer business models, huge investments ($ 2.4 Billion in year 2019 in India), Technologically enabled start-ups posed an opportunity as well as challenge to the organizations. Collaboration has helped organization to bring in lot of efficiency in terms of service levels, visibility and better decision making with help of technology. We must build supply chain parallel to reach the efficiency level or collaborate to leverage their expertise and deliver better customer experience.

Warehousing Mangement

3.1 Definition

Warehouse is a physical infrastructure for storage of goods with value added activities to ensure the product availability at right time in desired quantity. Warehousing plays an important role is supply chain though traditionally it was looked down as a wastage, but modernization has led to role change and now called as Fulfilment centres. It plays critical role not only in managing the demand, service levels but over a period it has become differentiator as well.

e.g.- IKEA unique supply chain model, the warehouse fulfils multiple roles in one. Differentiator as it reduces one leg of supply to distributor or retailer, multiplies as showroom cum display centre not only storage etc.

Types of Warehouses:

Warehouses can be categorized into 3 types:

- a. **Ownership Based**
- b. **Function Based**
- c. **Technical Requirement Based**

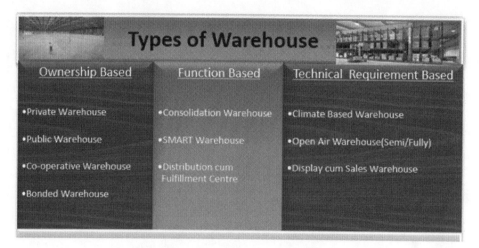

Exhibit-8: Types of Warehouse

Comparison of various Warehouse Types:

Type of Warehouse	Ownership	Functions	Characteristics
Private	Private/ Company	Storage and Supply	Long Term/Strategic Hiring
Public	Govt Owned	Storage and Supply	Low Cost/Temporary hiring
Co-operative	Co-operative Organization	Storage and Supply	Available on Cost basis (Mostly Not for Profit) to support members and non-members in business
Bonded	Govt Owned	Time bound Transition Storage facility	Used for storing Imported Items/ Avoids duty to be paid till paperwork completes
Smart	Private/ Company	Bulk Breaking/ Packing/Storage and Supply	High Automated Warehouse for quick Order fulfilment for large volumes
Consolidated	Private/ Company	Storage and Supply	Demand based flexible warehouse space/Economical/Mostly 3PL Owned e.g.- Cargo Companies warehouse like DHL/GATI

Type of Warehouse	Ownership	Functions	Characteristics
Distribution Centre	Private/ Company	Bulk Breaking/ Packing/Storage and Supply	Mostly built with specific requirements and storage is for shorter duration e.g.- Amazon Warehouses
Climate Controlled	Private/ Company	Storage and Supply	Temperature/Humidity based requirements e.g.- for keeping perishable goods or products, Dairy Industry/Frozen Foods
Open Air (Semi/Fully)	Private/ Company	Storage and Supply	Used for Bulk storage of voluminous products which are less prone to pilferage in open or semi open facility e.g.- Fully Open air- Storing of Building material/ Metallurgical Items (Pipes, wires, sheet etc), Semi Open Air – e.g.- Container based open storage
Display cum Sales Warehouse	Private/ Company	Storage, Display/Sales and Supply	Multipurpose warehouse which works as Storage cum display warehouse e.g.- IKEA Warehouse

Exhibit-9: Warehouse Function and Characteristics

3.2 Warehouse Selection Criteria

As per market estimated there will huge investments in coming 5 years for Integrated warehousing. So, warehouse selection is an iterative and exhaustive process. We can largely divide in the whole process in 4 steps-

Warehouse selection Process:

- Step 1
- Step 2
- Step 3
- Step 4

Exhibit-10: Process for Warehouse Selection

Author's Tip- To recall the process remember NEAD-R (Pronounced as NIDAR) process to take decision judiciously than perception-based process

WAREHOUSE ASSESMENT CHECKLIST	
(a) NEEDS IDENTIFICATION	
Warehouse Required	☐ New Location ☐ Relocation in same city ☐ Additional Space in Existing Area
Period	☐ Short Term ☐ Long Term
Ownership	☐ Owned ☐ Leased ☐ 3PL Managed
Area Required	
Preferred Location	
Purpose	☐ Storing ☐ Labelling ☐ Packing/Bulk Breaking ☐ Consolidation
Specific Requirements	☐ Climate controlled ☐ High Throughput ☐ High Safety ☐ Scalability ☐ Others If any
Availability	☐ Within 30 Days ☐ Within 180 Days ☐ > 180 Days
Documenting the Attributes & Specifications	Define required Attributes and Specifications of warehouse {Refer Section (b) for details}

WAREHOUSE ASSESMENT CHECKLIST	
(b) ATTRIBUTES AND SPECIFICATIONS	
Warehouse Type	☐ Open Air ☐ Semi Covered ☐ Fully Covered ☐ Climate Controlled
Warehouse Design	☐ U Shaped ☐ I Shaped ☐ L Shaped
Property Type	☐ New /Custom ☐ Running Condition ☐ Need Repairs
Roof Condition	☐ Concrete ☐ Pre Fabricated Sheet
Roof Height	☐ 18-24 ft ☐ 25-30 ft ☐ 31- 36 ft ☐ > 36 Ft
Roof Specification	☐ Thermal Insulation ☐ Natural Light ☐ Ventilation system
Floor Type	☐ Concrete ☐ Pavement ☐ Soil ☐ Others
Facilities	☐ Office Space ☐ Security Guard Cabin ☐ Parking Space ☐ Restroom ☐ Running Canopy ☐ Sufficient Bays ☐ Secured Boundary ☐ Green Area/Garden ☐ Fire Hydrant ☐ Play Arena ☐ Wide Passage Area ☐ Vertical Space for racks ☐ Controlled Entry/Exit ☐ No Blind Spots ☐ Dock Levellers ☐ Washroom/Bathroom ☐ Kitchen ☐ Dining Area ☐ Change Room ☐ First Aid Kit ☐ Drinking Water ☐ Server Room ☐ Conferecne cum Meeting Room

WAREHOUSE ASSESMENT CHECKLIST	
(b) ATTRIBUTES AND SPECIFICATIONS	
Access To	☐ Access to Highway ☐ Access to Railway Siding ☐ Access to Airport ☐ Access to Port ☐ Labour Availability ☐ Internet Access ☐ Mobile Connectivity ☐ Electricity ☐ Nearby Fire Station ☐ Hospital & Ambulance ☐ Transport Hub ☐ Nearby Hotels and Motels ☐ Public Transport ☐ Garbage Disposal Area ☐ Fuel Station ☐ Vehicle Service Centre
Risk Profiling	☐ Flood Risk ☐ Pilferage Prone Area ☐ Labour Union ☐ Political Interference ☐ Stubble Burning ☐ Unauthorized Construction ☐ Scalability and Temporary Storage ☐ No Overhead High Tension Wires ☐ Insufficient Turning Radius in Warehouse ☐ Narrow Approach Road for Warehouse ☐ Unsafe storage facility adjoining the warehouse ☐ Ground Water Pollution due to nearby Indutries ☐ Air Pollution due to nearby Indutries
Environment (Green Enabled)	☐ Water Harvesting ☐ Day Time Illumination ☐ Arrangement for Storing Hazardous Goods ☐ Solar Light System ☐ Paper Recycling Facility

WAREHOUSE ASSESMENT CHECKLIST	
(c) Decision Making and Conclusion	
Initiate RFQ	☐ Technical Bid ☐ Finacial Bid
Shortlisting & Finalization	☐ Lowest Bidders ☐ Negotiation ☐ Reverse Auction
Legal Verification and Agreement Signing	☐ Legal Verification ☐ Joint Finalization of Terms and Conditions ☐ Registration of Agreement
Resource Mobilization	☐ Infrastruture ☐ Manpower ☐ IT Connectivity ☐ Registration & Complaince ☐ MHE Deployment ☐ Transporter and other vendors Deployment ☐ Information to Stakeholders ☐ Training to Staff ☐ Stock Shifting
Start of Operations	
Review & Realign	☐ Infrastruture ☐ Risk Profiling

3.3 Warehouse Design & Flow

Design of Warehouse:

Warehouse designs can be decided based on three factors

a.   Space Requirements
b.   Throughput requirements
c.   Resource Utilization (Manual/Semi Auto/Automatic) like Manpower and Equipment's

Warehouse Design for material flow can be categorized broadly in three type:

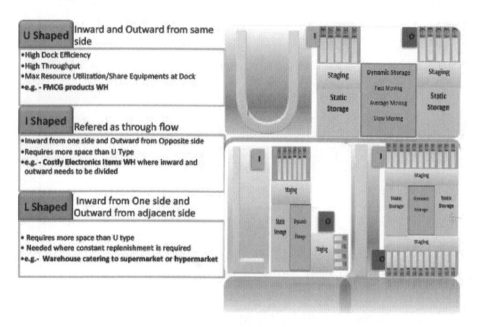

U Shaped	Inward and Outward from same side

• High Dock Efficiency
• High Throughput
• Max Resource Utilization/Share Equipments at Dock
• e.g. - FMCG products WH

I Shaped	Refered as through flow

• Inward from one side and Outward from Opposite side
• Requires more space than U Type
• e.g. - Costly Electronics Items WH where inward and outward needs to be divided

L Shaped	Inward from One side and Outward from adjacent side

• Requires more space than U type
• Needed where constant replenishment is required
• e.g.- Warehouse catering to supermarket or hypermarket

Exhibit-11: Warehouse Material Flow Design
(I-Inward and O-Outward Flow)

3.4 Warehouse Resource Selection and Process Optimization

Warehouse Characteristic changes based on the objectives, SKU being catered, functions being performed, Throughput and velocity required, Vertical height usage etc. Warehouse Resources selection is vast topic which is critical to ensure the right cost and optimum service level which is covered in brief. Resources for warehouse can be broadly divided in three categories:

a. **Manpower-** To be decided based on Throughput/Shift Workings/SKU Type

b. **Working Capital Requirement-** To be managed based on Cash vs Credit terms with Vendors and suppliers.

c. **Material Handling Equipment's-** Handling equipment's has primarily three roles to play in any warehouse (1) Capacity Enhancement in terms of throughput and vertical storage (2) Improve product velocity in warehouse (3) Safety of Man and Material

To be decided based on the design flow, Type of SKU, Throughput requirements, Safety Issues and Vertical Height Uses like Hand pallet trucks, Battery Operated Pallet Trucks, Forklifts, Scissor Lift etc. For Automated warehouses it will be the length of conveyor belt, automated picking robots/Packaging Machines and Sorting Machines will be required.

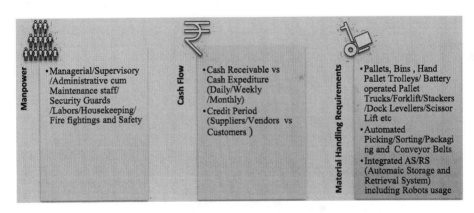

Exhibit-12: Warehouse Resource Selection

Warehouse Process Optimization:

Warehouse resource selection will lead to efficiencies and productivity. Warehouse resource optimization goals must be defined in advance to ensure objectives are achieved in desired manner.

Optimize each process being performed in the warehouse for resource optimization:

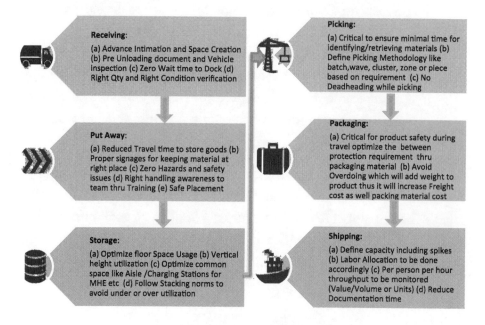

Receiving:

(a) Advance Intimation and Space Creation (b) Pre Unloading document and Vehicle inspection (c) Zero Wait time to Dock (d) Right Qty and Right Condition verification

Picking:

(a) Critical to ensure minimal time for identifying/retrieving materials (b) Define Picking Methodology like batch,wave, cluster, zone or piece based on requirement (c) No Deadheading while picking

Put Away:

(a) Reduced Travel time to store goods (b) Proper signages for keeping material at right place (c) Zero Hazards and safety issues (d) Right handling awareness to team thru Training (e) Safe Placement

Packaging:

(a) Critical for product safety during travel optimize the between protection requirement thru packaging material (b) Avoid Overdoing which will add weight to product thus it will increase Freight cost as well packing material cost

Storage:

(a) Optimize floor Space Usage (b) Vertical height utilization (c) Optimize common space like Aisle /Charging Stations for MHE etc (d) Follow Stacking norms to avoid under or over utilization

Shipping:

(a) Define capacity including spikes (b) Labor Allocation to be done accordingly (c) Per person per hour throughput to be monitored (Value/Volume or Units) (d) Reduce Documentation time

Exhibit-13: Warehouse Process Optimization

3.5 Warehouse Performance Metrics

Quality	Responsiveness	Financial/Cost	Productivity
Put Away Accuracy	Warehouse Order Processing Time	Total Warehousing Cost	Storage Space Utilization
Picking Accuracy	Put Away Time	Product Damages -In House	Units Handled per Hour
Manhour Loss			Non Storage Area

Quality Indicators

1. Put Away Accuracy

Definition

It measures the no of items placed in correct bin or location in warehouse or storage area

Formula

$$\text{Put Away Accuracy} = \frac{\text{No. of Units Correctly Placed}}{\text{Total No. of Units}} * 100$$

2. Picking Accuracy

Definition

It measures the no of items/lines picked correctly in terms of quantiy and Item in warehouse or storage area

Formula

$$\text{Picking Accuracy} = \frac{\text{No. of Units /lines Correctly Picked}}{\text{Total No. of Units/Lines}} * 100$$

3. Manhour Loss

Definition

It measures the no of incidents/accidents happened in a defined period of time finally leading to loss of manhours

Formula

$$\% \text{ Loss of Manhour} = \frac{\text{No. of manhours lost}}{\text{Total No. of Manhours Worked}} * 100$$

Responsiveness Indicators

1. Warehouse Order Processing Time

Definition

It measures the amount of time taken to process the order from the date and time it is received in warehouse

Formula

$$\text{Warehouse Order Processing Time} = \frac{\text{Order Shipped Date \& Time - Order Received Date \& Time}}{\text{Total No. of Orders Executed}}$$

2. Put Away Time

Definition

It measures the amount of time taken to place the material from staging area to storage area per consigment basis. It determines the productivity of the team involved for the task

Formula

$$\text{Put Away Time} = \frac{\text{Total Time Taken to Store the material from Staging}}{\text{Total No of Consignments}}$$

Financial/cost Indicators

1. Total Warehousing Cost

Definition

It measures the total cost incurred in running the warehouse for specific time period

Formula

$$\text{Total Warehousing Cost} = \frac{\text{Warehouse Rental Cost + Manpower Cost+ Utilities Expense + Equipment's Rental + Consumables + Miscellaneous}}{\text{Average Value or Unit of Inventory Stored for time period}}$$

2. Product Damages -In House

Definition

It measures the value of damaged material over a period of time (Quarterly or Annualy) against the total stock shipped . It determines the efficiency of storage measures taken to keep the material in good condition

Formula

$$\text{\% Value of Damages} = \frac{\text{Total Amount of damages in Warehouse}}{\text{Total Value of material Shipped}} * 100$$

Productivity Indicators

1. Storage Space Utilization

Definition

It measures the utilization of the total space available for storage in terms of volume within specified time. The space occupied by a units is called Cubic Index which can be calculted based on their volume requirement plus stacking norms of each SKU.

Formula

$$\text{\% Capacity Utilization} = \frac{\text{Storage Space Utilized in cubic feet}}{\text{Total Space available in Cubic Feet}} * 100$$

2. Units Handled per Hour

Definition

It measures the no of units/Boxes or pallets moved per person per hour in warehouse or storage area during inward and outward both

Formula

$$\text{Per Capita Units Handled} = \frac{\text{No. of Units /Boxes/Pallets moved}}{\text{Total No. of hours worked / No of persons}} * 100$$

3. *Non Storage Area*

Definition

It measures the percentage of space which is not being used as storage space and assigned for other works like aisle space/Charging area/Packaging area/meeting room etc.

Formula

$$\text{\% of Non-Storage Space} = \frac{\text{Non-Storage space in Cubic ft}}{\text{Total Space in Warehouse (Cubic ft)}} * 100$$

Inventory Mangement

4.1 Definition

All materials and goods kept in warehouse by an organization for future demands is called **Stock.**

List of all items kept in stocks by an organization is called **Inventory**

All aspects and processes leading to control the stock(s) is called Inventory Management

Note - An **Item** is a distinct product kept in stock.

Types of Stock:

Stocks can be broadly categorised in 3 Major Categories and 2 Minor Categories

Major Category is classified based on the status of material namely-

a. **Raw Material Stocks**
b. **Work In Progress (WIP) Stocks**
c. **Finished Goods Stocks**

Minor Category is based on their Utilization in the **SIMOC** Process

a. **Consumables like Oil, Paper, Cleaners etc.**
b. **Maintenance, Repair and Overhaul (MRO) Stocks**

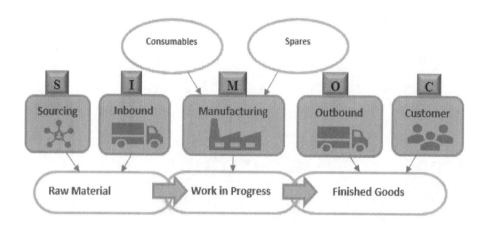

Exhibit-13: Warehouse Process Optimization

Note -Apart from this the stocks can be classified based on objectives like Safety Stock, Seasonal Stocks, One Shipment Stocks, Pipeline Stocks etc.

4.2 Approaches to Inventory Control

Inventory Control approaches can be defined as policy guidelines or decisions made for the stocks like

a. What needs to be kept in stock?
b. How much cost to be incurred?
c. What should be the Days of Stocks?
d. When to replenish/Re-Order?
e. What will be the best suitable safety stock?

The above questions throw the complexity to decide on the Inventory which is required to meet the demand at optimum cost. Decision making needs to happen at three level:

a. **Strategic decisions:** are most important, have effects over the long term, use many resources and are the riskiest. These set the overall direction for operations- **e.g. To be shipped directly to customer from plant or Keep stock in warehouse to cater demand**

b. **Tactical decisions:** are concerned with implementing the strategies over the medium term, they look at more detail, involve fewer resources and some risk **e.g. Items to be stored/ How much to Invest in Holding Inventory**

c. **Operational decisions:** are concerned with implementing the tactics over the short term; they are the most detailed, involve few resources and little risk. **e.g., Order Size for coming month**

Above decisions will have to be taken in cohesion with the organizations Mission, vision, values and Objectives. Also, one must keep in mind the strategy (As per Michael Porter) adopted for the doing the business:

a. **Cost Leadership**- Competitive product to customer at lesser cost

b. **Product Differentiation** – Differentiated product to cater the customer requirements.

c. **Niche Segment**- Exclusive and premium product for selected customer

To elaborate further on Decision Making one can consider one or more factors (Sample below) in practical world for warehousing:

Factor	Objective	Benefit
Timings	Reduced Lead Time	Improved Cash to Cash Cycle/Less Obsolescence
Customization	Product and Volume	Improved Customer Satisfaction/ Less Demand Supply Gap

Factor	Objective	Benefit
Diversified Offering	Wide Range of offering from fulfilment centre	Better Customer acquisition rate/ Better Profits
Resource Optimization	Operations/Value addition at low cost	Economies of scale leading to profit

4.3 Inventory Management Techniques

Inventory management is very complex and challenging task to be performed. It has direct impact on Customer satisfaction, Loss of value due to mistakes in receiving and shipping, Sales loss due to Stock outs, Safety issues due to poor storage etc. We can divide the whole task of managing inventory in three aspects:

a. Storage Norms
b. Quality of storage/stocks and Sustenance
c. Inventory Movement – Safety of Stocks/Right Pick up-Ship Up/Freight Cost Management

Storage Norms	Quality Of Storage	Inventory Movement
☐ EOQ (Economic Order Quantity)	☐ ABC Analysis	☐ MOQ (Minimum Order Quantity)
☐ Safety Stock Inventory	☐ VED Anlysis	☐ Cross Docking
☐ Re-Ordering Point	☐ SDE Analysis	☐ Bulk Shipment
☐ Demand Forecasting	☐ FSN Analysis	☐ One Shipment
☐ JIT (Just In Time)	☐ FIFO (First In First Out) /LIFO (Last In First Out)	☐ Periodic Inventory Count
☐ Dropshipping	☐ Lean Six Sigma	☐ Perpetual Inventory Count
☐ Consignment Inventory	☐ Batch Tracking	

Economic Order Quantity (EOQ)- EOQ tool is used to optimize the Inventory. It can be used to define different production intervals or Order Levels thus minimizing costs associated with buying, supplying and storing. It works on assumption that when the Inventory volumes rise the cost of Ordering goes down while at the same time the cost of Holding Inventory goes up. EOQ is the qty which gives the best output.

$$\text{EOQ (In Units)} = \sqrt{\frac{2*\text{ Demand (In units) * Order Cost (Per Order)}}{\text{Holding Cost (Per unit /Per Year)}}}$$

Step -A **No of Orders** = D (Annual Demand Qty)/Q (Quantity Per Order)

Step -B **Annual Ordering Cost**= D/Q * Ordering Cost (Fixed in Nature)

Step -C **Holding Cost**= Carrying Cost (Interest on Money Invested to Hold the Inventory) * Unit Cost

Step-D **H (Average Holding Cost)** = Q (Quantity/2) * C

Step-E **TC (Annual Total Cost)** = Annual Ordering Cost +Annual Holding Cost

$$\text{Total Cost} = D/Q*S + Q/2 * H$$

$$\text{EOQ (In Units)} = \frac{dTC}{dQ} = \sqrt{\frac{2*D*S}{H}}$$

Author's Tip- EOQ does not consider variability in Holding cost or Ordering cost which makes is less relevant where seasonality or skewness brings the cost variability

Safety Stock Inventory- Safety stock Inventory is the additional stocks being kept to avoid stocks out or in case of highly variable demand or adjust the forecasting errors

Re-Ordering Point – Re-Order point considers the lead time and safety stock for to place the order for restocking. This is to ensure stocks outs due to lead time and avoid loss of sale

Demand Forecasting- Mostly based on historical data and demand trend and the stocks are kept based on prediction. Demand Forecasting happening in real time is an effective tool to keep the inventory optimum and avoid obsolescence.

Just In Time (JIT) – A well-known technique to reduce Inventory Costs. Inventory is Received from suppliers in sync with planned production schedule. It's needs based supply and ensures no dead stock

Drop shipping- An order fulfilment method that does not require a business to keep products in stock. Instead, the store sells the product, and passes on the sales order to a third-party supplier, who then ships the order to the customer

Consignment Inventory- When consigner agrees to pay the consignee goods meant for sale but the consignee pays only when the stock is sold then the arrangement is known consignment Inventory

ABC (Always Better Control) Analysis- An important tool to ensure right decisions are to store the products. Its derived from Pareto analysis and categorizes the inventory in 3 categories

1. **Class A (Critical Products)**- High Value/High Quality/High Profit margin but contributes to 20% in total Inventory but 80% of Revenue
2. **Class B (Medium class Products)**- It stands in between the critical and trivial product category. Normally it contributes to 30% of total Inventory and 15% of revenue
3. **Class C (Trivial Many Products)**- Low value/low revenue products fall in this category. They contribute 50% of total Inventory and 5% of total revenue. But they are essential and vital for overall profit but individually don't matter much

VED Analysis- VED stands for Vital, Essential and Desirable and is qualitative in nature unlike ABC which is quantitative. It's mainly used for spares based on the functionality of the part.

SDE Analysis- SDE sands for Scarce, Difficult and Ease in terms of availability. Its mainly used in spares, imported items and raw material

FSN Analysis- FSN stands for Fast moving, Slow Moving and Non-Moving. The analysis is done where large stocks are kept, and it starts blocking capital due to slow movement or non-movement of stocks.

FIFO/LIFO- FIFO stands for First In -First Out and LIFO is Last In First Out. As the name suggests two strategies are used when avoiding the obsolescence or remove the inflation issue. FIFO is normally used to avoid obsolescence and keep the ageing stocks minimal or Nil like food/Apparels etc. However, LIFO is used where product value increases with time normally Supermarkets,/Pharmacies/Coal/Wines are fine examples

(*Note – FEFO and LEFO is used by industries where Expiry is an area of product Quality like processed foods/Medicines etc*)

LEAN SIX SIGMA- It's a vast subject which focuses on set of tools, philosophy and a system to reduce the inventory levels and bring standardization in the Inventory management process. It basically works on demand management, Cost and waste Reduction, Process Standardization, Industry standardization, cultural change, and cross enterprise collaboration to bring efficiencies. 5S, Kanban, Kaizen, DMAIC methodology are known principles for implementation. (*Refer Chapter -6 for more details on Lean SIX SIGMA and the principles*)

Batch Tracking- Batch Tracking refers to a specific set of products based on specific information like supplier details, manufacturing location, expiry date, Specific shifts and helps us to track the following (a) Track Expiry dates (b) Track Returns and pinpoint the defects happened in which set of products (c) Gives accurate costing and quality details for each set

Minimum Order Quantity (MOQ)- MOQ is the quantity defined by the organization to optimize the cost associated with movement. Typically used in traditional distribution models wherein the inventory is supplied to Wholesale Dealers and Retailers for selling. It will vary based on product to product and geographical demand pattern as well.

Cross Docking- Cross Docking is an activity within warehouse which happens for fast paced business where products are shipped with no time lag and with minimum storage time i.e.- except staging and sorting for onward distribution or supply there is no inventory in warehouse. The Inflow and outflow movement of Inventory is almost equal in terms of qty/pallets/packages on overall basis where inflow happens in bulk then sorting happen for supply in smaller lots based on demand. It ensures higher throughput; better inventory turns and no obsolescence. The model must be designed in such a way that pace remains equal for inflow and outflow. Any mismatch will create bottleneck in the overall supply chain.

Bulk Shipment- Bulk shipment refers to transportation of goods in large quantity most often in unpacked condition like iron ore, petroleum products, grain, coal etc.

(Break Bulk is also synonymous sounding word, but it differs as the movement happens in unitized way like in terms of pallets, bagged, strapped form or in non-utilized form like vehicles etc)

One Shipment: One shipment is normally used when all the material is required in one go based on customer demand and/or site complexities to avoid storage at site. Organization must source material from all supplier/manufacturing plants and store till every product is received in desired numbers and ships at customer place/ project site in one go.

Periodic Inventory Count: Periodic Inventory count is done after specific interval to assess the accuracy of the inventory rather than doing it after every sale. It determines the ending qty and cost of goods sold.

Perpetual Inventory Count- Perpetual system uses cycle counting method on day-to-day basis to assess the exact ending inventory post the days transactions are over. It helps us in maintaining accuracy of the stocks kept in warehouse and reduces disruption in operations.

4.4 Replenishment Models and Sectoral Approach

There are basically 2 approaches to replenishment:

a. *Fixed Order Quantity Replenishment Model* (**Q model**)– Stocks are replenished with a fixed quantity at varying interval levels once the stocks deplete to certain predefined level.

b. *Periodic Review Replenishment Model (P model)*-Stocks are replenished at periodic time interval in variable quantity to reach to the targeted level of quantity.

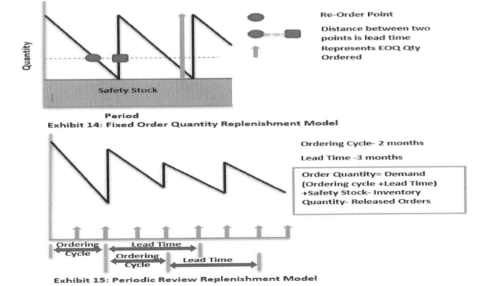

Exhibit 14: Fixed Order Quantity Replenishment Model

Exhibit 15: Periodic Review Replenishment Model

Difference between Q system and P System		
Factors	Q System	P system
Order Trigger	Stock reaches to Reorder Points	At fixed review period, not stocks level
Period of Order	Any time based when stock reaches to reorder point	At predefined time interval
Order quantity	Reordered qty remains constant	Reordered qty varies each time
Inventory Size	Less than P system	Larger than Q system
Control Method	Perpetual count method	Periodic count Method
Record Management	Needs to be maintained each time as stock movement happens	Only during review period

Exhibit-16: Difference between P & Q replenishment systems

4.5 Performance Metrics for Improving Visibility

Quality Indicators

1. Inventory Accuracy Rate

Definition

It measures the accuracy of System Stocks (WMS/BIN Card/Ledger) vs physical stocks available in storage area

Formula

$$\text{Inventory Accuracy Rate} = \frac{\text{No. of SKU's/Units Correctly Matched}}{\text{Total No. of SKU's / Units}} *100$$

2. Stock Wastage Ratio

It measures the percentage of stocks is non usable due to expiry or damage in overall inventory stored over a period of time

Formula

$$\text{Stocks Wastage ratio} = \frac{\text{Value of stocks in non-usable condition}}{\text{Total Value of stocks stored}} * 100$$

3. Stock Out Rates

It measures the percentage of sku's which faced stock out leading to loss of sales against the total SKU's stored over a period of time

Formula

$$\text{Stock Out ratio} = \frac{\text{No of SKU's went out of stock}}{\text{Total no. of SKU's stored in}} * 100$$

(The same can be measured that a SKU has faced stock out situation in percentage of facilities for the organization or an average no of stock outs experienced for a SKU over a period in a facility as well)

4. Order Fill Rates

It measures the percentage of all orders placed in storage facility (ies) are fullfilled/delivered correctly out of all orders palced over a specified period of time at at any point in the supply chain

Formula

$$\text{Order Fill Rates} = \frac{\text{No of orders fulfilled correctly}}{\text{Total no. of Order placed}} * 100$$

Responsiveness Indicators

1. Order Lead Time

It measures the amount of time taken to fullfill the order from the time of receipt in the storage facilitiy within specific period

Formula

$$\text{Order Lead Time} = \frac{\text{(Order fulfilled Date/ time – Order Received Date/time)}}{\text{Total no of orders processed}}$$

2. Order TAT

Order Turaround Times measures the amount of time taken to fill the order i.e. the time taken to pick/pack, load and documentation.It can be calculated over a period of time to understand the time spend in each activity and remove bottlenecks

Formula

$$\text{Order TAT} = \frac{\text{Time taken to process orders over a period}}{\text{Total no. of Orders Processed in the period}}$$

Financial Indicators

1. Inventory Holding Cost

It measures the the cost expediture done irrespective of their nature for a period of time mostly annual. The cost may include Rentals of property and equipments, Utility Bills, Taxes, Insurance Cost, labor, security, housekeeping cost, loss due to damage/pilferage, other administrative costs, Capital expenditures, etc

Formula

$$\text{Inventory Holding Cost} = \frac{\text{Total Annual Holding Cost incurred}}{\text{(Capital + Non-Capital)}}$$

2. Unaccounted or Lost Stock Cost

It measures the total value/Units of stocks which is either lying unaccounted or phsyically missing from the inventory. It results in loss of sales and helps in decision making for replenishment to cater demand

Formula

$$\text{Unaccounted or Lost Cost of Goods} = \frac{\text{Value/Units of stocks unaccounted or lost}}{\text{Total Value/Units of stocks}} * 100$$

3. Order Fullfillment Cost

It measures the cost incurred on fullfilling per order from the warehouse which includes all process costs like manpower expenses, Stationary charges, communication/coordination expenses , Equipment rental, Consumables, Employee welfare cost , safety arrangement cost Miscellaneous expenses etc over a period of time.

Formula

$$\text{Order Fulfillment Cost /Order} = \frac{\text{Total Cost incurred in Fulfillment of Orders}}{\text{Total no. of Orders Processed}}$$

Productivity Indicators
1. Inventory Turns

Inventory turns measures that how many times an average inventory has been sold from storage/Warehouse/Distribution centre or fullfillment center. Higher the turns , better the effciciency as it reduces the holding cost, obsolescence cost etc

Formula

$$\text{Inventory Turns} = \frac{\text{Total Value/Units of Inventory Sold}}{\text{Average Value/Units of Inventory stored}}$$

2. *Perpetual/Periodic Counting*

It measures the percentage compliance adherence against the total defined counting frequency to ensure the accuracy and mitigate the risk asscoated with mismatch in stock over a period of time (Daily/Monthly/Annually)

Formula

$$\% \text{ Adherence to Stock Counting} = \frac{\text{No of times Inventory counting done}}{\text{Total no. of times Inventory Count Planned}} * 100$$

Digitalization: Latest Trend & Practices

Digital is defined as "using a system that can be used by a computer and other electronic equipment, in which information is sent and received in electronic form as a series of the numbers 1 and 0" (Cambridge Dictionary)

Digitalization can be defined as using the digital means to store, view or perform an activity in secure and easy way through connected platform(s) like cloud and Internet.

So, the question remains why Digitalization is important? The answer lies in the current trends which has started dominating the Supply chain like High flexibility, adjustments and quick adaptability to cater change in demand levels, Consistent quality required from customer and optimizing the cost has led to creation of newer business models, latest technologies being deployed for visibility in real time and proactive approach to avoid disruption. There are lot of disruptors which are summarized below:

Compliance-In Indian context post GST a lot of compliances has changed to ensure that the business entities are required to get registered. Also, e-way bill has been introduced for time constrained completion of the transaction. Recent development ensures that the Invoices are generated thru govt controlled portal with a QR code.

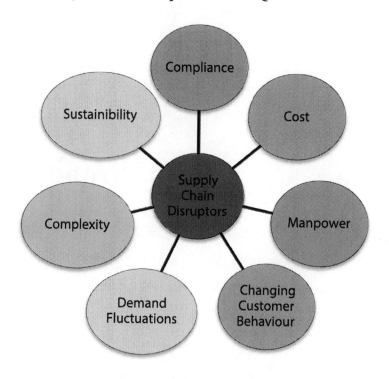

Exhibit-17: Supply Chain Disruptors

(Recent amendment and unification of archaic Labour laws into four major laws has given the flexibility for business to operate in comfortable way but puts a huge risk in case of non-compliance whether its social security benefits or workplace safety)

Cost: As industrialization started and we moved into high GDP growth, but the infrastructure development moved at snails' pace and so the associated ecosystem required for the logistics and warehousing sector. We are still operating in double digits i.e. 14% when it comes to logistics cost to GDP. Our average road travel speed in less than 40km/hour on national highways which is far lesser than trucks potential. *Apart from infrastructure volatile demand, high customer expectations, high* *return ratio and cost, non-value-added activities add to woes in big way.*

Manpower - Acquisition cost for ready to serve the in-logistics sector is very high and being mostly unorganized it creates a lot of bottle necks for even efficient organizations. In recent times the supply chain and logistics professionals have gain importance but still there is big gap in supply and demand. Also, when it comes to decision making its still less of analytics and more of experience or trend based. *High fluctuations in demand requires high flexibility in manpower deployment which becomes cumbersome to manage and lead to many issues like cost escalation, safety, efficiency per capita, speed of operations etc.*

Changing Customer behaviour: This is the change, which is permanent, but the rapid speed of change has led to serious disruption in the supply chain domain in recent years. Whether expectations of consistent quality, lesser wait times or Post Covid safety precautions requirement all has significantly challenged the status quo. Organizations are still facing challenges to keep the consistency in offline and online modes in terms of cost, delivery times and safety requirements. *In nutshell customer wants effortless delivery at their terms and conditions in all interactions which is herculean task.*

Demand Fluctuations: Despite analysing the data through statistical models, buying pattern studies and many more ways to predict the demand, fluctuations have become more severe and uncertain. *Seasonal fluctuations, Heavy discounting by e-comm companies put a severe pressure on the ecosystem, bullwhip effect, reduced product life cycles, fast technological advancements*, increasing purchasing power and demand from tier II and tier III cities where still the logistics ecosystem is developing disrupts the supply chain in big way.

Complexity: Multi-echelon decision making, multistage processing and controls, disperse geography, High no of SKU and their changing demand pattern, Suppliers collaboration in real time basis, stiff competition and many more such things make the supply chain a very complex and cumbersome thing to manage. As these factors grow the complexity grows manifold

Sustainability: Sustainability has gain prominence in current times. Customers are becoming concern over ecological impact and preferring green energy usage and products even. SO, supply chains must become proactive like optimize the fossil fuel usage, using recycled papers for packaging to minimize the same. More usage of clean fuel driven commercial vehicles, less kilometre's travel per product are the key challenges.

In the Post Covid Scenario digitalization has taken a leapfrog jump and acceptability to the change is at all-time high. Also, the e- commerce platforms and their dominant usage of digital means esp. in logistics has brought focus of traditional industries to the benefits which can be accrued by adopting the digitalization.

Digitalization in the supply chain/value chain has led to concept of Industry 4.0 (4th Industrial Revolution) sometimes called synonymously to Digitalized supply chain. Basically, an approach where Physical and Digital world are connected and complement each other while working parallelly.

Industrial 4.0/Digitalized Supply chain/SMART Manufacturing works towards automation and taking the best use of both worlds i.e. Physical and Digital. The interfaces supporting this smooth interchange of data, information and further processing of activities in automated way can be listed as below as per BCG and Deloitte:

Digital Ecosystem	Attributes (*What it offers*)	Support (*What it improves*)	Application (*Where it is used*)	Examples
Big Data Analytics (BDA)	Processing Variety and Volumes of Data with Velocity	Decision making, Predictive Analysis, Prescriptive Analysis	Manufacturing, Retail, Logistics, Healthcare etc	Surge Price Mechanism deployment from Uber and Ola with help of **BDA**
Augmented Reality (AR)	Lively Visual Experience, Interactive, Mobility, Enhanced and deeper Customer connect beyond physical boundaries	Cost Efficiency, Productivity Improvement, Higher ROI	Medical Training, Education, Retail, Tourism Industry, Advertisement and Entertainment Business	**Smart AR** Glass for warehouse which shows the location of material to be picked and shortest route
Additive Manufacturing (AM) [3D Printing, Binder Jetting/ Material Jetting/ Power Bed Fusion/Sheet Lamination/ Direct Energy Deposition]	Rapid Prototyping, Direct Digital Manufacturing, Easy to setup and easy to manufacture, Mobile Manufacturing	High product Customization, Reduced Complexity, Precision, Flexibility and speed to produce in easy way	Medical (Body Parts Making like ear), Consumer Products, Aerospace, Automobiles, Defence Industry, Supply chain	**Lifestyle products** like shoes, glass, watches, jewellery, furniture printing

Digital Ecosystem	Attributes (*What it offers*)	Support (*What it improves*)	Application (*Where it is used*)	Examples
Cloud Computing (Infra as a Service-IaaS/ Platform as a Service-PaaS Software as a Service-SaaS)	Scalability, Reliability, Flexible Pay Structure, Security	Reduced Capital Expenditure, Cost Savings, Easy accessibility to data in real time, Mobility	Applicable to all Industrial Setup where data needs to store, retrieved and analysed with safety	Few renowned players are Google, AWS, Microsoft/IBM/ Oracle etc facilitating cloud computing to all industries
IOT (Internet of Things) or **IIOT** (Industrial Internet of Things) **IOMT** (Internet of Medical Things)	Machine to Machine (M2M) Communication at multiple level and responses/action, Devices are Connected through internet/ Software	Reduced Human Intervention, Improved Productivity and operational Efficiency, Reduced Downtime, Better Occupational Safety, Reduced Downtime of Equipment's	Manufacturing, Transportation, Oil and Gas, Healthcare, Agriculture, Power Transmission and distribution	**IOMT**-Real time **health monitoring of Patients** like heart rate, BP, Oxygen level etc **IIOT-Transportation** real time tracking of vehicles and real time rerouting, **IOT based smart Barcode readers** which are connected to ERP for tracking Inventory movement leading to better control **IOT-** Wearable smart watch, Home automation & Smart TV all connected to Mobile device

Digital Ecosystem	Attributes (What it offers)	Support (What it improves)	Application (Where it is used)	Examples
Vertical and Horizontal Integration	**VI**-Highly standardized processes and interfaces within Organization **HI**-In build interface and connected systems with suppliers and even up to POS/customers	Better Efficiency, Optimized Cost, Real Time data driven decision making and Business Intelligence, Uniform and Unitized digital setup	Applicable to all Industrial Setup working in silos and drive driven decision making	**Horizontal Integration-** Reliance Retails buying Future Group retail business Flipkart buying Myntra **Vertical Integration-** Its within organization to break silos.
Simulation	Seamless Collaboration among various teams across geographies in **Product Development**, **Digital Mock Up** for faster and better decision making at low cost **Discrete event Simulation** offers micro level analysis of each operations	Fast decision making, Risk mitigation at Low cost Quick data sharing and correction in design making or layout finalization situations, Innovative Solutions for real life problems in advance	Primarily all Precision Manufacturing set up, Design centric based organizations	All Industries like **Aerospace,** Oil Sector, Defence Industry, **Space Technology oriented organizations** where taking risk in real time is very high and costly
Autonomous Vehicles	No or Reduced Human Intervention, Better Safety for Operational Team	Reduced work force, Optimum resource Utilization	Manufacturing setup, Warehousing, Last mile delivery	All Manufacturing Organizations, Warehousing Organizations

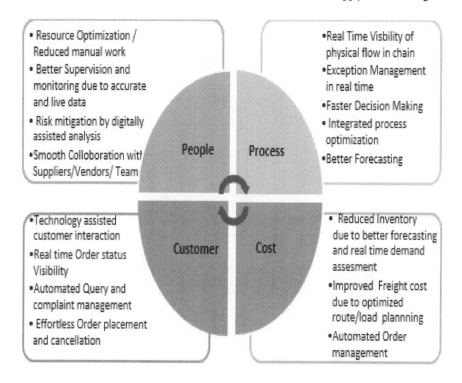

• Resource Optimization /
  Reduced manual work
• Better Supervision and
  monitoring due to accurate
  and live data
• Risk mitigation by digitally
  assisted analysis
• Smooth Colloboration with
  Suppliers/Vendors/ Team

• Real Time Visbility of
  physical flow in chain
• Exception Management
  in real time
• Faster Decision Making
• Integrated process
  optimization
• Better Forecasting

People   **Process**

Customer   **Cost**

• Technology assisted
  customer interaction
• Real time Order status
  Visibility
• Automated Query and
  complaint management
• Effortless Order placement
  and cancellation

• Reduced Inventory
  due to better forecasting
  and real time demand
  assesment
• Improved Freight cost
  due to optimized
  route/load plannning
• Automated Order
  management

Exhibit-18: Advantages of Digitalization

Solution lies in deploying the **Cyber Physical systems** to ensure that the supply network operates un-interruptedly and effectively. These physical and digital systems work as cohesive unit in the value chain(s) to ensure smooth information and communication.

The digital systems deployed must be uniform, unified, and connected, to process all desired tasks of complex supply chain network.

Being a very vast and rapidly evolving domain, benefits are immense and has been explained in brief on key points only. When we talk of latest trends which are emerging and taking shape are many and will be touched in brief for familiarization. Few of them are as follows:

Control Towers: Control towers are latest trend and has become popular after successful deployment from **major e-comm players like Flipkart/ Amazon etc.** Major role includes:

Exhibit-19: Control Tower

1-Visibility: Supply Chain visibility is big task and mostly a lacking one in the organization. There are multiple steps which are required to create visibility in the overall supply chain.

a. Data Feed (Deploy digital means for easy data feed)
b. Data Consolidation and Processing (Auto Consolidation thru software)
c. Dashboards, Presentations -Mobility with Security
d. Alerts on Exceptions and Corrective action from control tower

2-Data Analysis and Forecasting-(a) Descriptive analysis based on pre-decided metrics data is processed in auto mode and gives required visibility on controls points like reason of success or failure. **(b) Predictive analysis** ensures scenario planning based on statistical modules and investigates the reasons which helps in minimizing the risks and improving supply chain efficiency by predicting the events. **(c) Prescriptive analysis** with advent of AI and big Data analytics the systems analyse and not only gives information of events likely to occur but prescribes suitable actions as well to mitigate risk

3-Collaboration and Integrated Optimization- Horizontal (Between Suppliers and Customers)/Vertical (Between supply chain partners and competitors) and Network model collaboration (Consists of all stakeholders and works on the principle of Co-opetitition) The collaboration leads to an Integrated Optimization of all supply chain functions to make it resilient and effective

(**Co-Opetition**- Cooperation with Competition to leverage the strength of each other and create efficiency in overall supply chain).

> **Author's Tip**- Basic planning for control tower should start with what we want to Track, Measure and Control (Refer Metrics of Supply Chain /Logistics and Inventory) and at what level (Granularity to be decided) and move to deploy digital resources to get the data and move up in the ladder towards visibility, predictive analysis and Integrated Optimization thru collaboration.

Blockchain: Blockchain is a kind of digital ledger kept in the form of strings (Cryptic form) and controlled by nods (computers) across geographies. **Its distributed** (Due to Peer-to-Peer Network), **immutable** (Due to Consensus algorithm from nods), **verified and secure** (Through Digital Signatures and key which is in string form). Below Exhibit-20 depicts the formation of blocks and many such blocks coming together making a block chain

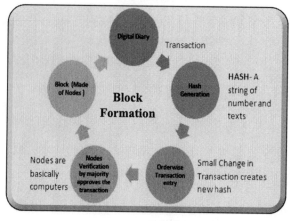
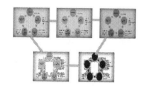

Multiple Blocks form a closed network cum chain which is called Blockchain

Exhibit-20: Formation of Blockchain

Use of Blockchain in supply chain/value chain is much talked subject and has long term implications due to its USP. Few practical examples are digital approval of shipments and tracking in secure way but accessible to all stakeholders including Customs, Port authorities, consignor, consignee and agents. Another example is in healthcare sector esp. for high value medicines where it can track from manufacturer to consumer by using the Blockchain including payment.

Digital Twins and Digital Thread: Digital Twins is a concept where digital devices interact with Physical system and not only monitors, collects data, store it but analyse it to give valuable insights which can lead to improving productivity, reducing wastages and cost optimization. It's much more capable than CAD (Computer Aided Design)/IOT (Industrial Internet of things) and deploys/uses various hardware's (like Sensors/Pressure Monitors) and software's including AI for visibility, analysis, data modelling and prediction cum prescription.

"A digital twin can be defined, fundamentally, as an evolving digital profile of the historical and current behaviour of a physical object or process that helps to optimize business performance"

- Deloitte University Press

Digital Thread concept started from military aircraft industry and now being used in Industrial manufacturing process. It is a common link (process or activity or attribute) which connects digitally across complete product life cycle i.e. from design, development, manufacturing to Quality check. It helps in creation of digital twin for optimizing business performance by near real time visibility and analysis.

Digital Service Providers and Business Models:

As digital technology is still evolving as well as its application in various industries and processes. One needs to be very cautious but not ignorant in deployment of platforms which will facilitate the existing processes in terms of efficiency, wastage reduction and faster decision making. So, how to approach for the digitization is very important and critical for successful transformation. There are three dimensions with respect to implementation: **Software (b) Hardware (c) Amalgamation**

a. **Software:** The digital tool or programme which is going to be used for generating, processing, recording, predicting, and analysing any data and activity for the user is called Software

b. **Hardware:** Any internal or external devices being used to run the Software and perform the desired task are called Hardware. The Basic equipment needed is a Computer and can range from Bar Code Scanners to Digital Sensors in the Supply Chain.

c. **Amalgamation:** A very crucial part in the journey of **Digitalization** is planning the seamless integration with existing set-up for optimum leverage of the tools and technologies deployed. Any misfit or poor integration will lead to huge loss or cost escalation for rectification.

Digital Technology Service Providers: The service providers will be basically working on the above three dimensions either providing solutions for one part or mix one or in integrated way.

Software Service Providers (SSP): A company will be providing the software which can be installed/integrated with the existing set-up or installed with new device for a task. **e.g.**- An application which can be installed (DIY) for CRM solutions or Complaint Tracking etc Few companies like Salesforce, ZOHO, Freshworks works on this mode and provide complete CRM solution etc.

Hardware & Service Providers (HSP): A company providing the physical device(s) to run the software and helping it perform the desired activity can be called as Hardware Service Providers. **e.g.**- Computer supplying organizations like Dell, Apple etc or suppliers of routers, switches, Servers, sensors, Optical Fibre cables etc will come in this domain.

Hybrid Solution & Service Providers (HSSP): A company may offer Hardware as well as software as a complete package for an activity or task. **e.g.-** Bar code scanners/Temperature sensors monitoring, Air Quality monitoring and Display. Scanners and Sensors have inbuilt software programmes to read, record and display which is supported by a physical device recording data and providing visibility.

Currently a lot of such HSSP have come into existence and provide need based, customized and standalone solutions to organizations.

Integrated Digital Solutions & Service Providers (IDS&SP): Its bigger in comparison to HSSP and has holistic view to look at a problem and offers complete package for making the process or activity digitally enabled. It plays primarily a role of Collaborator with accountability and may take support from SSP/HSP/HSSP to give best possible solution. **e.g.-** An organization offering to setup control tower for the organization will collaborate with SSP/HSP/HSSP to provide a complete solution and with guaranteed performance cum service level which will be fulfilled by keeping a constant monitoring and maintenance of the Software and Hardware deployed. Few companies like Tech Mahindra, TCS and IBM can be categorised as IDS&SP.

Introduction to Lean Six Sigma

"Six Sigma Methodology is a set of business tools, statistical theory, and quality control knowledge that helps improve your business procedures. It has the capability of improving performance while decreasing process discrepancy"

(Six Sigma Council)

Lean Six Sigma is concept which emphasizes on reducing wastages (Refer Chapter 1-Section 4 for wastages of Supply Chain) and improvise to work as Value chain where every function adds some value to it. To do so it deploys various qualitative and quantitative measures to analyse and improve each function of the value chain. A brief introduction to few key concepts, tools and techniques will be covered-

1. **DMAIC Methodology**: One of the most important and widely used tool for improvement. It stands for Define, Measure, Analyse, Improve and Control.

Step 1- Define	-Identify the process/Parameter to be improved -Understand impact on business/customers (VOC) -Define Team and timelines -Make a Charter to track Progress

Step 2- Measure	-Identify Tools and Technique to gather data -Define Parameters for Input, Process and Output
Step 3- Analyse	-Create Problem statement -Work on Root Cause Analysis -Implement Process Controls -Analyse the deviation from standards defined -Identify Scope of Improvement
Step 4- Improve	-Brainstorm Ideas for solution -Create Roadmap for the Best Solution and expected outcome -Communicate Changes to process stakeholders -Implement the Solution
Step 5- Control	-Verify the results as targeted -Alter the course (Process) in between (if required) -Record Learning and share

2. **RASCI Matrix:** RASCI Stand for **Responsible, Accounted, Supported, Consulted & Informed**

Responsible: The person who is on the ground to act and perform to complete the task

Accountable: Person who is liable for the outcome. Normally one person is in this category for the task.

Supporting: Person or persons assisting the team for task completion but directly not effected by milestones or outcomes

Consulted: Person or team who has the experience, exposure or expertise is asked to advice based on requirement.

Informed: Those who needs to be updated on the task progress

3. **FMEA (Failure Mode Effects Analysis):** FMEA is a risk proofing methodology and being done proactively to take correctives in advance to minimize the loss. It considers three dimensions to analyse the risk primarily in the Process (PFMEA) or Design (DFMEA):

   a. **Occurrence:** This considers the probability of the risk coming to fore in the process or design. A numerical value is assigned ranging between 1-10 where 1 is the lowest probability and 10 being the highest.

b. **Severity:** It looks over the factor about the loss or delay or wastage happening if a particular risk occurs in the process or design. A numerical value is assigned ranging between 1-10 where 1 is the lowest probability and 10 being the highest.

c. **Detection-** What are the chances to detect the deviation or anomaly in the process/design is factored and measured. A numerical value is assigned ranging between 1-10 where 1 is the Highest probability of deviation getting detected and 10 being the hardest to detect the problem.

Post assigning value to each risk on these factors, RPN (Risk Priority Number) is defined as follows-

RPN (Risk Priority Number) = (Occurrence*Severity*Detection)

Post RPN number is calculated the focus must be on the higher values to avoid serious lapses or breakdown.

4. **Poka-Yoke:** Poka-Yoke (Literally means "avoid inadvertent mistakes"). It is very vital for error proofing. The methodology works in three ways-

a. **Shut Out strategy** – The process or function is designed in such a way that eliminates the risk **e.g.** Let us take an example of Moving mechanical part used for cutting. In shut-out strategy the machine is equipped with sensor so if the any body part touched accidently the machines is auto switched off

b. **Control Strategy-** It is designed in such a way that the process stops if there is mistake **e.g.** In this strategy the moving part of the machine will be placed in such a way that body parts cannot touch the machine when working. Another example is *DIY products where there is numbering or design instructions to be followed to make the product else it cannot be assembled.*

c. **Attention Strategy**: It brings your focus before doing the task **e.g**. *In this method there will be visual warning placed at the safe limit to make the operator aware about the danger zone he is approaching*

Other examples –

a. ***Tagging or stickering the lot or barcoding*** *them at the point of origin to avoid wrong routing or wrong delivery* ***(b) Checklist for Vehicles*** *to ensure that there is no water leakage or any protruding bolts etc which may damage the product during in transit* ***(c) Auto shut off Nozzles at petrol pump*** *to avoid safety issues* ***(d) Colour coded stickers on the Products*** *(based on the batches or month of manufacture). It helps in ensuring the FIFO/LIFO guidelines while dispatching and you pick based on your requirement* ***(e) In racks there are limit switches*** *which are used. There is constant noise till the operating gate is closed so that someone does not fall from there.*

5. **Kaizen:** It consists of two words **Kai- Change & Zen- Good**. A concept which focuses on continuous improvement is called Kaizen and it works with various tools and methodologies to improve the process. It focuses to utilize mind hours of each one involved in the process and challenge the status quo. Five Basic Principles are as follows (As per Kaizen Institute)-

a. *Know Your Customer*
b. *Target Zero Waste*
c. *Be Transparent*
d. *Empower People*
e. *Go to GEMBA (Be at the Point of Action)*

What it Targets to Improve:
MUDA- Wastages
MURA-Unevenness/Fluctuation
MURI-Over-processing/Over-Burden/Unreasonable

Exhibit-21: Example of MUDA/MURA/MURI

6. **5S/6S**- It is a tool use by Japanese to ensure maximum efficiency and reduce idle time due to poor work-floor management. It consists of 5 terms starting with S and are as follows:

Sort (Seiri)	Segregate the machine, material as per their status and dispose off the non usable ones e.g. (a) Segregate Finished Products and Spares (b) Perishble vs No perishble
Set In Order (Selton)	Arrange the in sytematic manner and preferably homgenous in terms of visuals and defined objective e.g Fast moving items kept together
Shine (Seiso)	Define cleaniness frequency, process adopted for ensuring hygiene and tracking the same including light arragments e.g. Tracker display which monitors the cleaning frequency
Standardize (Seiketsu)	Make the activity process driven to create uniformity in the practices followed every time and each place e.g. Shadow Boards for keeping tool in manufacturing set up
Sustain (Shitsuke)	Ensure training, awareness and audits to ensure that process arein place and being followed. Ultimately it should reach to a stage of self discpline
Safety (Anzen-Sei)	All 5S activities must lead to safe workplace and no downtime due to hazard and accidents

Exhibit-22: 5S/6S Process Chart

7. **JIT (Just in Time)**-Just in Time is a philosophy which was conceptualized and adopted by Toyota Production systems to ensure that the materials are made available at the time of requirement. It basically works on reducing Inventory Holding cost and improved working capital flows. The concept encompasses and uses a lot of tools, technique and methodologies to achieve this.

8. **KAN BAN-** KAN BAN term roughly translates to Visual Card/Sign Board/Billboard and supports the JIT concept. It's a scheduling process where in a Physical Card/Digital display ensures proper visibility at each processing point. Display ensures that the material is indented timely which will avoid stockouts or overstocking by reducing the wastages in manufacturing setup. It follows the concept of Pull for production to optimize the manufacturing process and give more value to customer at lesser expense. Kan Ban can be used in many other ways like keeping track on progress of projects **e.g.** Selection of new site for Warehousing can be tracked as shown in Exhibit 23

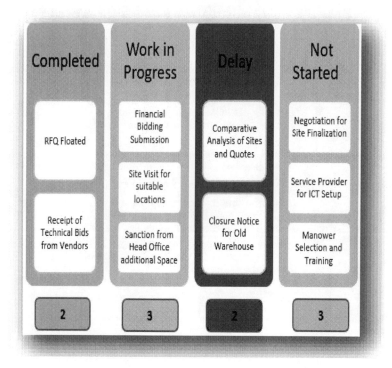

Exhibit-23: Warehouse Site Selection

9. **Cause Effect Diagram (Fish Bone Diagram)- Also known as Ishikawa Diagram,** Cause effect Diagram basically tries to find the root cause of the given problem in detail. It primarily focuses on but not

limited to primarily 6 factors namely Man, Machine, Material, Money, Method and Environment. It is simple to use and qualitative in nature.

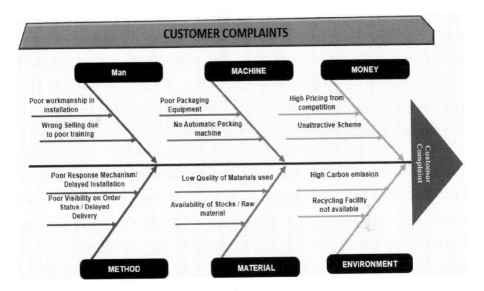

Exhibit-24: Cause Effect Diagram -Customer Complaints

10. **Pareto Analysis:** Introduced by Italian economist Mr Vilfredo Pareto in 1906 and further used by Mr Dr Joseph Juran for Industrial use in 1940's. This tool is alternatively called 80:20 rule, the law of vital few/Useful many/trivial many as well. This is very simple but strong statistical tool for decision making. It works on the principle that the 20% of factors contribute to 80% of effects. **e.g.** 20% of products contribute to 80% of the profit or 20% of the line produces 80% of the total defects during manufacturing. It can be analysed by Pareto Chart or Diagram to understand the factors. Sample is given below for Customer Complaints.

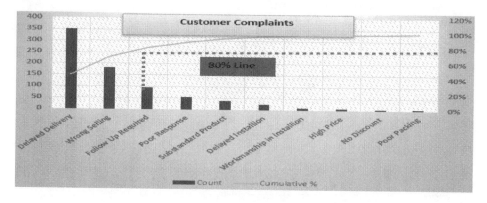

Exhibit-25: Pareto Analysis -Customer Complaints

11. SMED (Single minute Exchange of Die)- Developed by Shigeo Shingo, the process focuses on reducing the changing time of Die in during production. It works on the flexibility and standardization of the process. It literally doesn't mean that the change time must be a minute but emphasizes on to reduce the current times and bring it to single digit of minutes. Such flexibility gives opportunity to quickly shift the production and shadow the demand. Technically it helps in reducing the Mura factor (Unevenness) in Manufacturing. (*The process follows the shifting from process of Internal Set-up (Change happens when Production line is down) to External Setup (Change can happen when line is up and running) and work to reduce the Internal Set up Timings*)

12. OTED (One Touch Exchange of Die)- This is next level of SMED which focuses on highly level of precision, avoiding screws/fasteners and usage of clamps for change of dies. In simple terms in single step the exchange should happen and avoid wastage.

13. SHABD* (Single Hour Arrangement Based on Demand)- It reduces to avoid one of the wastages i.e. **Wait Time** during the supply chain process esp. on logistical arrangement. {**Refer Chapter 2, Section 4 (e)**} (**Note-**Authors Method to deal with uncertainty in Logistical Arrangement)

14. **TAKT TIME**- It can be defined as the amount of time taken to complete a process or set of processes. For calculation Takt Time is equal to the total time available for the process completion divided by Demand received from Customer. E.g. Let's assume we have demand of 50 units from customer per day and total available time (Reduce Lunch time, breaks, meeting etc) is 8 hours. So, the Takt time is equal to (8*60)/50 =9.6 Min or 576 seconds.

15. **ANDON**- Andon is Japanese term for Paper Lantern. This follows the methodology where with the help of tools or display mechanism the problem or the status of a process is communicated in terms of quality. In Nutshell, the production line alarms the executives, managers and other stakeholders in case of any deviation from the set objective manually or automatically. It may be through text message, email notifications, Alarms, Lights or Visual Board on the floor or even in high automatic setup it will stop the process.

16. **JIDOKA**- Jidoka is an important tool and base pillar for lean concept. It emphasizes on the elimination of the root cause of the problem once caught and then only resume the process which ensure the quality is inbuilt in the process itself. The detection should be autonomous in nature and process should stop till it gets corrected. Aim for deployment of this method in manufacturing with the help of ANDON is to ensure that defect is noticed and rectified immediately, and no further build of defective stocks happen. *One of the simple examples of JIDOKA is Printer in office. If the toner gets empty the printer doesn't work and red light automatically start signalling about the issues*

17. **HEIJUNKA**- Heijunka simply refers to Levelling esp. in production setup. It works on the predictability, flexibility and stability of the production process. It uses a variety of tools and methods to implement

this and works towards to achieve the status "Batch size of One" in true sense. To name a few tools which helps towards Heijunka are SMED/OTED/TAKT TIME/KAN BAN etc. It minimizes the wastage which happens in Batch Size Production as customer demands are fluctuating in nature.

18. **GEMBA WALK-** Gemba is Japanese word which translates to "actual place". It works on the principle of what is focused upon that improves and for focusing one must be at the place of action e.g. Shop floor in manufacturing. It's a very systematic and planned approach to find inefficiencies, good practices alike which will give impetus for realigning resources and process. The main aim of this method is to bridge the gap between perception and actual action happening at the place of action.

19. **GEMBITSU-** Gembitsu is Japanese word which translates to "actual thing". It is next part of improvement starting with GEMBA. You must focus on actual thing where the observation or improvement has to happen. Let's say the quality of the product in a manufacturing plant. Managers must focus on the quality conformance which is predefined in the process and in real.

20. **GENJITSU-** Genjitsu is the action which follows post facts are analysed post Gemba walk and Gembitsu. Managers must incorporate the ground realities while taking decision on the important aspects in the improvement journey.

Note- Gemba, Gembitsu and Genjitsu are called 3G strategy in Kaizen Process. It focuses for "hands on approach" before decision making for executives and managers

21. **5 W (WHY-WHY-WHY) Analysis-** An iterative step which keeps on asking questing in probing manner till the main root cause is not found.

5 Why doesn't mean that the process should not end at 5 why but it keeps on repeating till there is one problem which has cascading effect on the problem. The *Loop must continue* **Question- Answer- Question** *till one final Answer comes*

22. **Control Charts:** Control Charts are an important statistical process control tool for keeping a view on the process status whether it's in control or not as per the defined criteria. It defines the Upper control limit (U.C.L.) and Lower Control Limit (L.C.L.) for a process and track the status and fluctuations. It quickly gives a signal of the trouble areas and deviations occurring against the defined limit. **e.g.** Let assume that we need to understand the fluctuation happening and Control range for material being supplied at a distance range of 250-350 kilometres on Cost per unit basis (Total Cost Incurred/Total Units Supplied). Below exhibits explains the working and the typical control chart will look like

Control Chart (Individual –Moving Range):

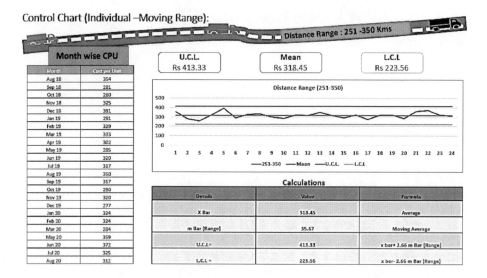

Month wise CPU		U.C.L. Rs 413.33	Mean Rs 318.45	L.C.L Rs 223.56

Month	Cost per Unit
Aug 18	354
Sep 18	281
Oct 18	260
Nov 18	325
Dec 18	391
Jan 19	291
Feb 19	329
Mar 19	333
Apr 19	302
May 19	285
Jun 19	320
Jul 19	317
Aug 19	350
Sep 19	317
Oct 19	290
Nov 19	320
Dec 19	277
Jan 20	324
Feb 20	324
Mar 20	284
May 20	359
Jun 20	372
Jul 20	325
Aug 20	312

Calculations

Details	Value	Formula
X Bar	318.45	Average
m Bar (Range)	35.67	Moving Average
U.C.L =	413.33	x bar+ 2.66 m Bar (Range)
L.C.L =	223.56	x bar– 2.66 m Bar (Range)

Exhibit-26: Control Chart

Another important aspect of control chart is to interpret correctly to diagnose the issue and take correctives. A typical look at the data will throw four dimensions:

a. **Threshold State**- Process in control but some non-conformance

b. **State of Chaos**- Process Out of Control and Some non-conformance

c. **Brink of Chaos**- Process Out of Control but 100% Conformance

d. **Ideal State**- Process in Control and 100% conformance

These stages will not remain until and unless monitored and improved time to time. At some stage it will fall back in State of Chaos.

Another important factor in reading control chart is **7-point consistency** which can be in four situations

   a.   **7 points above average limit**
   b.   **7 points Below average limit**
   c.   **7 Point going consistent upward from average limit**
   d.   **7 point going consistent downward from average limit**

Such situation indicates of a problem which is hidden and the data points as well as the process needs to be checked for any anomaly despite the line remaining within control limits.

Above explained LEAN Six Sigma methodologies and tools can be utilized on standalone basis or as a mix of it in systematic manner to achieve the objective of the error free, process based and for consistent quality output.

References

https://www.researchgate.net/figure/Supply-and-Demand-Chain-Comparison_tbl2_228789428

http://carl.sandiego.edu/itmg350/types_of_supply_chain.htm

https://www.tocinstitute.org/theory-of-constraints.html

https://www.whatissixsigma.net/seven-types-of-waste/

https://dspace.mit.edu/handle/1721.1/34869#:~:text=Within%20this%20architecture%2C%20supply%20chain,chain%20costs%20within%20an%20organization.

https://hbr.org/2007/08/building-a-resilient-supply-ch%20May%2011

https://hbr.org/?id=4176BN&&referral=2430

https://cscmp.org/CSCMP/Educate/SCM_Definitions_and_Glossary_of_Terms.aspx

https://www.michiganstateuniversityonline.com/resources/supply-chain/is-logistics-the-same-as-supply-chain-management/

https://www.supplychain247.com/article/10_rules_for_supply_chain_logistics_optimization

https://www.gartner.com/en/newsroom/press-releases/2019-10-14-gartner-identifies-5-actions-to-optimize-logistics-cohttp://www1.ximb.ac.in/users/fac/visiting/vfac.sf/23e5e39594c064ee852564ae004fa010/89b99a7daf20080665257086002ecac4/$FILE/Product%20and%20Process%20Design%20-%20RG.ppt

https://www.mhlnews.com/transportation-distribution/article/22054501/the-abcs-of-activitybased-costing-for-logistics

https://www.dhl.com/in-en/home/our-divisions/supply-chain/thought-leadership/infographics/eight-trends-disrupting-logistics-transportation.html

https://www.accenture.com/_acnmedia/PDF-53/Accenture-Digital-Disruption-Freight-Logistics.pdf#zoom=50

https://www.pwc.com/sg/en/publications/assets/future-of-the-logistics-industry.pdf

https://www.forbes.com/sites/insights-penske/2018/09/04/the-4-forces-transforming-logistics-supply-chain-and-transportation-today/#6bfe4a89b752

https://www.ey.com/Publication/vwLUAssets/ey-disruption-digitalization-disintermediation/$File/ey-disruption-digitalization-disintermediation.pdf

https://www.itln.in/indian-transportation-and-logistics-startups-attracted-24-billion-in-2019-report

https://siam-shipping.com/warehousing-management/

https://www.tradegecko.com/blog/supply-chain-management/ikeas-inventory-management-strategy-ikea

https://www.logisticsbureau.com/the-7-principles-of-warehouse-and-distribution-centre-design/

https://www.shippingandfreightresource.com/check-points-to-choose-the-right-warehouse-for-your-products/

https://www.who.int/biologicals/expert_committee/Supplement-1_TS-warehouse-site-ECSPP-ECBS.pdf

http://deliver.jsi.com/dhome/resources/publications/allpubs/pubsfortopic?p_persp=PERSP_DLVR_TOP_SCE

https://www.bigcommerce.com/blog/inventory-management/

https://mahindralogistics.com/technology/control-tower

https://www.forbes.com/sites/stevebanker/2019/06/05/north-american-railroads-need-to-do-better/#5174c7943214

https://www.mckinsey.com/business-functions/operations/our-insights/supply-chain-40--the-next-generation-digital-supply-chain#

https://scribewriting.com/parts-of-book/

https://blog.mpo.com/3-types-of-supply-chain-control-towers

https://link.springer.com/chapter/10.1007/978-3-319-56345-9_3

https://www.cognizant.com/perspectives/how-a-digitized-supply-chain-control-tower-can-make-your-value-chain-soar

https://www.sdcexec.com/software-technology/article/10289792/
supply-chain-strategies-to-manage-volatile-demand

https://www.bcg.com/capabilities/operations/digital-supply-chain

https://www.researchgate.net/publication/317567258_Trends_and_
Strategies_in_Logistics_and_Supply_Chain_Management_-_Digital_
Transformation_Opportunities/link/593ffe3eaca272876dc4fb62/
download

https://www.plextek.com/insights/insights-insights/industry-4-0-and-
the-9-pillars/

https://www.idashboards.com/blog/2019/07/31/the-pillars-of-
industry-4-0/

https://www.ssrn.com/index.cfm/en/engrn/

https://www.allerin.com/blog/4-ways-the-supply-chain-industry-will-
use-augmented-reality

http://www.apics.org/sites/apics-blog/thinking-supply-chain-
topic-search-result/thinking-supply-chain/2018/11/05/five-ways-
augmented-reality-supply-chain-management

https://www.inc.com/james-paine/10-real-use-cases-for-augmented-
reality.html

https://additivemanufacturing.com/basics/

https://www.journals.elsevier.com/additive-manufacturing

https://www.lboro.ac.uk/research/amrg/about/
the7categoriesofadditivemanufacturing/

https://www.datacenterdynamics.com/en/news/gartner-defines-five-
attributes-of-a-true-cloud-service/

https://www.scribd.com/document/412689296/Gartner-Research-
Cloud-Computing-Planning-Guide-2019

https://usa.kaspersky.com/resource-center/definitions/what-is-cyber-
security

https://iiot-world.com/industrial-iot/attribute-based-encryption-
could-offer-huge-benefits-to-the-iiot/

https://www.i-scoop.eu/internet-of-things-guide/industrial-internet-
things-iiot-saving-costs-innovation/industrial-internet-things-iiot/

https://www.pwc.com/sk/sk/odvetvia/assets/global-industry4-0.pdf

https://amfg.ai/2019/03/28/industry-4-0-7-real-world-examples-of-digital-manufacturing-in-action/

https://www.sciencedirect.com/science/article/abs/pii/S0959652616316675

Digitalization in Supply Chain Management and Logistics Smart and Digital Solutions for an Industry 4.0 Environment by Prof. Dr. h. c. Wolfgang Kersten, Prof. Dr. Thorsten Blecker, Prof. Dr. Christian M. Ringle

https://blog.kainexus.com/improvement-disciplines/six-sigma/dmaic/a-step-by-step-walkthrough-of-the-dmaic-process